Y0-BUT-586

FIVE YEARS IN CHRISTIAN SCIENCE

BY

WILLIAM W. WALTER

PUBLISHED AND FOR SALE BY
WILLIAM W. WALTER
564 NEW YORK STREET
AURORA, ILLS.

TO MY DEAR WIFE, WHO YET DARED TO HOPE WHEN ALL SEEMED HOPELESS TO ME, AND WHO WAS THE CHANNEL THROUGH WHICH GOD, INFINITE LOVE, SPOKE THE DIVINELY INSPIRED WORDS "TRY CHRISTIAN SCIENCE," I LOVINGLY DEDICATE THIS BOOK.

PREFATORY NOTE.

All people who are blessed of God to be channels for good to their fellow-men are thankful and are moved by an impulse which is divinely natural to let their light so shine before men that they, seeing the good work, may glorify not the worker, but our Father which is in heaven. With this thought in mind, the title of this book is a sufficient indication of the nature of its contents, and of the purpose for which it is written.

THE AUTHOR.

CONTENTS

FIVE YEARS IN CHRISTIAN SCIENCE

CHAPTER I

A cold winter morning; a sick man sitting dejectedly before a large hard-coal base-burner, bolstered up with pillows in an old-fashioned plush rocker; a woman, careworn and sorrow-faced from worry and from the fear that her husband would soon leave her never to return. The sick man is myself; the woman my faithful wife, who, with loving and anxious care, had done all in her power to make my burden less heavy; the time, February 12, 1905, following seven years of ill health, with the grim reaper—Death—supposedly but three days away. I noticed my wife observing me with more solicitude than usual as she passed back and forth in the room doing the housework. I was so weak that I could not walk without her aid, and so poverty stricken that we were at that very time living upon borrowed money.

As my wife finished the morning's work, she sat down in a chair by my side and tenderly asked: "Will, are you feeling worse than usual this morning?" It would have been useless for me to have answered in the negative, as my looks and actions would have belied my words; so I merely answered, "Yes." There was a silence lasting several minutes before my wife could control her feelings enough to speak to me again; then she simply said in a voice that she meant to be hopeful, but which sounded almost hopeless: "Let us try Christian Science; it may help you." Blessed words! although, then, I knew it not. I was slow in answering; so my wife continued, "You know Mrs. P——, the high-school janitor's wife?" I answered with a nod of my head. "You know that she has been an invalid for years, and that her case was considered hopeless." Another nod of the head was all the answer I made. My wife added: "She is well now, having been healed through Christian Science."

I heard the words, but made no sign that I had heard them, for I thought, "This may be true in Mrs. P——'s case, but my illness is something different. Besides, have I not tried the best physicians of my home town and also specialists from Chicago,—all with the same results?" After a time my wife spoke again: "Will, dear, let us try Christian Science, for I may as well admit, as you yourself already know, that nothing else has helped you, and now Christian Science is our last hope."

I knew nothing of Christian Science except from hearsay. I cannot say that I was prejudiced, as by nature I loved to take up new lines of thought and look into them; and had Christian Science been presented to me as a real science or philosophy I believe I would have given it a fair investigation. But truly the subtlety of the one evil is great in holding that which he claims as his own, so that both times, previously, when Christian Science was brought to my attention, it was presented to me in a very ludicrous light. The first time that I remember having heard the name, Christian Science, was twenty-three or twenty-four years ago. A man whom I knew well was hitching a span of mules to a street-car, when he accidentally caught his thumb between the clevis-pin and the bumper of the car, and bruised it terribly. At once he grabbed the injured thumb in his other hand, and, because of the pain, rocked his body violently to and fro, standing first on one foot and then on the other. I was yet some distance away when I saw a lady stop and talk to the man, and the next moment I saw him thrust the injured hand close up to the woman's face, and heard him say, in a very loud and angry voice: "You say that I did not hurt myself and that there is no sensation in matter! Look there! Look and see! I suppose you will say that that thumb isn't smashed and that I am only dreaming that it is aching and bleeding." I could not hear the quiet reply of the lady, but saw my friend turn abruptly from her with a look of disgust on his face. When I caught up with him, I asked what had happened and also who the lady was that had angered him. My friend replied: "That woman is one of those queer Christian Scientists, who believe that a man can't hurt himself because there is no sensation in matter, but I convinced her very quickly that she was mistaken."

The incident was so ludicrous and my friend's anger so genuine that I could not contain my laughter, and I laughed long and loud, and for some time afterward this incident was a standing joke between my friend and myself.

The second incident was of a somewhat similar nature, except that it was a case of stomach ache, and the man who complained of it was advised to try Christian Science for it. He asked the method, and was jokingly told to try to forget it, and the suggestion was made that they play a game of chess to aid him in doing so. The suggestion was taken, and the game of chess started; but after about five minutes' play the chessboard was pushed aside with the remark that he would like to see the man who could forget that he had such a pain as he had, whether he be a Christian Scientist or any other kind of scientist, and with the further remark that his ache was not an imaginary one, but a real one.

These incidents came vividly to mind, now that I was asked to try a remedy that I considered a joke; but because of my weakened condition, and the grave face of my wife, I answered, "I don't care. As we have tried everything else we might as well try this also." My wife did not give me a chance to change my mind, but hurriedly threw a shawl over her head and went to see the practitioner who had handled Mrs. P——'s case so successfully.

The practitioner agreed to call after dinner, and about one o'clock she came; and after a half hour's talk on Christian Science she silently gave me the first treatment. I recall now that I had very little interest in the matter in general, but was quite curious to know what the treatment consisted of and how given. I was surprised and a bit amused when I found that the treatment was only a silent prayer. Had not I prayed, with tears of pain running down my cheeks, times without number, and received no benefit therefrom? In my distress I began to wonder if God really lent a listening ear to those who call upon Him for help. (I was born and reared in a Christian home, and was a fairly regular attendant at church until the age of sixteen, at which time an occurrence happened that did much to change my thought,—in fact, from that time until I was married, six years later, I attended the Methodist, Baptist and Congregational churches more regularly than I did the church of my parents.)

And now, as I lay at death's door, a woman thought she could have me restored to health through prayer! However, I said nothing of my thoughts, but let the treatment go on, and also promised to read the literature that the practitioner had brought me. My wife was not in the room when the treatment was given, but later, as she came to understand somewhat of true prayer, she told me that she was in the adjoining room, praying as she had been taught, as rapidly as she could, hoping thereby to help matters along.

I read the three copies of the Christian Science Sentinel, and the copy of the Christian Science Journal left me by the practitioner that same day, and as I read testimonial after testimonial of what to me seemed miraculous healing, my thoughts were vacillating. First I would think of the testimonials in the light of the many patent-medicine advertisements that I had read; then the thought would come, "They are true, and if so, why might not I be healed by the same method?" Back and forth, between bright promise and black despair, my thought ran most of that first night. The second day was seemingly a repetition of the first, except that the practitioner asked me to get the Christian Science text-book, Science and Health, with Key to the Scriptures, by Mary Baker

Eddy, and bade me study it in connection with the Bible. I did not tell her that I never owned a Bible, but I promised to study as directed, but did not start the study of the Bible that day. The third day I had many questions to ask the practitioner, and in my anxiety to have them answered I entirely forgot that this was the day when, according to mortal reckoning, I was to have died.

The main question that I wished to ask was in regard to Jesus. To my thought he was a superhuman being, descended direct from a place above the blue-vaulted skies, which I had been taught was the location of our eternal home and which mankind call heaven. Imagine my surprise when the practitioner answered my query regarding Jesus with these words: "Mr. Walter, Jesus was a man, the same as you are, and it was what Jesus *knew* that made him the Christ and gave him power to heal all manner of disease and ultimately to triumph over death itself. Also, please remember that the Scriptures teach that the last enemy to be overcome is death, thereby showing us that death can be and should be overcome by all." The latter part of this statement did not at the time interest me nearly so much as the first part: that Jesus was a man the same as myself. Later, the force of the second part of the statement came home to me also, for, as I found myself rapidly getting well, what else was this work that was being done for me but the overcoming of death?

After the practitioner left me, her words, that Jesus was a man the same as I, kept running through my mind, and I determined to prove at once to myself the correctness or incorrectness of her words. So I asked my wife if she knew where we could borrow a Bible. She went to a neighbor's and got one for me. I started to read at the beginning of the New Testament, and was soon much interested in what I was reading; and as I read of the many healings accredited to Jesus the thought came: If Jesus really was a man the same as myself, then if I knew what Jesus knew I could also heal myself and others through this same *knowing.* I determined then and there to take it for granted that the practitioner's statement, that Jesus was a man the same as I, was correct, and I decided to read the Bible with the thought of finding out how and through what means Jesus did the healing. In connection with this determination I noted carefully both the words and actions of Jesus as related in the Scriptures, but still I arrived at no reasonable solution of the question.

The next day, the fourth day of my Christian Science experience, I secured a Science and Health, and read constantly all the day and evening, and on the fifth day I arrived at a portion entitled, in present editions of the text-book, "Mental Treatment Illustrated"; and through careful reading and thought I became aware of a little of the method of the application of Truth to the destroying of disease, and although I had proven nothing, I was satisfied that this was the method employed by the Master in his work. That very evening the opportunity came to try this method of casting out error (pain) with Truth, and I determined to follow the directions given in the text-book to the best of my understanding, and see what the result would be. My boy, then a lad of fourteen, had come to me complaining of an aching tooth, and, as it was after supper, his mother could not take him to the dentist, but she told him that on the morrow she would take him, and either have the tooth filled or extracted; but this waiting for the morrow was not very consoling to the boy, whose tooth was aching severely. It was then that the thought came to me to try the method explained in Science and Health,—not that I believed I knew all about it, but to try the little that I had apprehended. So I told my son to lie down on the couch and I would try to help him. I treated him for about fifteen minutes to the best of my ability, and then heard him get up from the couch, and, looking at him, I was much surprised to see him smiling, and, as he saw me look, he said, "Papa, the toothache is all gone." I was surprised, and also much disturbed. Was it the mental work which I had done that had stopped that raging toothache, or had it stopped of itself because the boy had lain quietly for a few minutes? I could not at once arrive at a satisfactory answer, but after some time I came to the conclusion that it could not have been the result of my work, because I knew so little of this method and had done so little in this case, but I was still much perplexed and thinking deeply.

I continued reading in Science and Health nearly all the night, it being about three o'clock in the morning when I finally, and with reluctance, laid this wonderful book down, so that I might get a few hours' sleep before daylight. I was up by six o'clock that same morning, and, as I was nearly through dressing, I reached for my glasses. I had been compelled to use glasses for a number of years, and needed to wear an extra pair of strong lenses back of my regular glasses if I wished to see well enough to read. While reaching for my glasses the thought came, "My eyes and sight as God made them are perfect, and therefore I don't need to wear glasses." I laid the glasses down again, and went down to breakfast without them, and as soon as breakfast was over I determined to treat myself for seeming imperfection of sight. Having this end in view, I picked up the Bible and tried to read. Here a little superstition crept into my thought, as I purposely selected the Bible to read from, thinking that God would prosper my work the more readily if I tried to read from the Bible. While I was not at the time aware of the futility of trying to bribe the infinite intelligence to quicker action by the holding of the Bible in my hand, it was not long thereafter that I discovered that Principle (God) never bends to conform to mortal thought, but that men must conform to His changeless law if they ever hope to gain that peace which passeth understanding. It was about half-past six in the morning of that memorable sixth day that I commenced my work for perfect sight, and—by constant mental work and carefully adhering to the instructions given in Science and Health—about four hours later I could see to read without the aid of any glasses, but still not as perfectly as I wished. By noon I could see very well. I scarcely took fifteen minutes for dinner, and then asked my wife if she could procure for me a Bible with smaller print, the Bible I had been reading from having very large print. She answered by saying that the people from whom she had borrowed the Bible I was then reading also had a very small one, and if I wished it she could get it for me. While she was getting the book I spent those few minutes in thanking God for the blessing already received, and prayed that it would be permanent.

When my wife handed me the little Bible and I had opened it and seen the tiny type, mortal mind (my belief) said, "You will never be able to read that fine print." In fact, the pages looked like a smooth, gray paper with a white border, but I had tasted of victory and I determined that I would win the whole battle before quitting my work.

For more than five hours I worked, declaring

the Truth as best I knew, with that Bible, with its mass of little letters, lying open in my lap. Sometimes I could distinguish a word and again I could not make out a letter. Then gradually the light came and I began to read, slowly, and a word at a time at first; then, after supper, I could see every word, although not clearly. I still continued my work, by alternately reading and treating myself, and, by two o'clock the next morning my sight seemed to be better than ever before in my life. But now I was afraid to stop my work for fear that I might have a return of the old condition, so I worked a few hours more, and then, with a heart overflowing with thanks, I sought my bed, after about twenty-two hours of constant work. I did not awake until nearly noon the next day, and from that day to this I have never felt the need of glasses, and frequently I read and study all day and most of the night.

When telling my friends of this demonstration I have been asked, "Did you do this work understandingly?" My answer has always been,

"A little understanding, a little faith, and much patience, won the day." I had read in the text-book, Science and Health, that "Patience must 'have her perfect work.'" At this time my entire mental and physical condition seemed to be undergoing a change, and I was noticeably stronger. The practitioner now asked me to call at her home for treatment and I complied, although the first visit taxed my determination greatly,—in fact, I consciously took the back streets so that none of my friends would know that I was visiting a Christian Science practitioner. Ashamed? No, I would hardly call it that, as my thought was, that if my friends should know they might joke me about it, and Christian Science had ceased to be a joke with me; and, knowing so little about it, I felt I would not be able to defend my position successfully.

A few days later I again had a chance to try my growing perception of this new science and was quickly rewarded, although the case was a simple nausea of the stomach. I treated it less than fifteen minutes and the trouble vanished.

At the end of twenty-eight days I was so far on the road to health that I told my practitioner that I would try to work out the rest of the problem alone, and my progress was rapid. The only thing that came to mar the peace of our household at this time was that my wife tried to dissuade me from any further study of Christian Science. My reply was that I was healed through this Science and that I proposed, if possible, to know just how it was done. She said: "Why do you need to care how the work was done? You are well and that is all that is necessary." It is only fair to state that, because of my constant study of the Bible, and Science and Health, my wife was afraid that I had become mildly insane on religious matters, and it was because of this, as well as the thought that I would leave entirely the religion of my childhood and embrace this new religion, as she termed it, that she tried to dissuade me from further study. But I had tasted of the fruits of Truth, and it was my nature to go to the bottom of all matters that I commenced to investigate, if such a thing was possible; therefore I said little, but studied the harder.

It was at this time that my wife's relatives began to notice the changed condition of my health and to remark about it, although they knew nothing of my taking treatment, as we had told no one. When they asked, I told my wife to tell them what had healed me and she did so gladly, because at their home was a sister that was suffering from what her doctors had told her was an incurable malady, saying that she would always need to take medicine for an affection of the heart.

When these good people heard the news of my healing they at once tried to persuade the invalid sister to go to a practitioner, but this she was loath to do. A few days later my wife decided to pay them a visit, thinking that perhaps the opportunity would be offered to say something that would induce the sister to try Christian Science, but she was not gone from our home more than a half hour before she returned. I at once asked the reason for her coming back so quickly, apprehending that perhaps she had not been well received on account of having mentioned Christian Science, but such was not the case, as her answer to my question clearly indicated. "Oh, I could not stay there any longer, for their house is much like a hospital this morning, and I heard nothing but complainings and sick talk, and I don't like to hear this kind of talk any more." I questioned her further, and she told me that the younger sister was lying on the couch suffering with nausea; that the older sister had caught cold, and the cold had settled in her throat and made her so hoarse that she could not speak above a whisper; and the third sister, the one that had been sick for years, was much worse than usual. Ordinarily I would have been somewhat alarmed at all this sickness, but even the little understanding of the nothingness of sickness that I had gained in my study of Christian Science enabled me in this instance to smile. My wife, observing me, said: "You need not smile;

they are really in trouble, and I wish you would go down and talk to them, for perhaps you can cheer them up a little." I asked her if she thought they would listen if I talked to them about the Christ, Truth, and she said she thought they would be glad to listen; so I decided to go.

I found the younger sister still lying on the couch in the living room in deep distress, while the other members of the family were just finishing their dinner. I talked to the young lady on the couch of the healing Christ, and after a little asked her if she wished me to try to help her. She answered in the affirmative, and I gave her treatment as best I knew, and with unbounded faith that she would be benefited. The treatment was of about fifteen minutes' duration, and, as I finished, the sick girl said, "I feel better already." I again talked to her of the wonderful healings accredited to Christ Jesus, and also told her of my own healing. The result was that by the time the other sisters had completed their dinner and came into the living room they found the sick girl sitting up very comfortably in an easy chair doing some needle-work. She greeted them with the words, "Girls, I am feeling better every minute." Of course, all wanted to know more of what had been done and how. I explained to the best of my ability the presence of all-powerful God, good, and before I left I was requested to treat the older sister for the cold, which I did. The response was not immediate and I was just a little disappointed, but said nothing, except that I would treat them again when I got home. The result came the next day and was quite complete, for, upon arising in the morning, the older sister could talk in her natural voice, and nearly all the soreness was gone from the throat, and the younger sister was up and around, seemingly none the worse for her experience of the day before.

Both of these sisters and my wife now began to importune the sister who seemed to have the incurable trouble to take treatment of me or from some regular Christian Science practitioner, but it was still several days before she would give her consent, as she thought that nothing would help her case. Had not she been told by one of our best physicians that her case was incurable? Besides, she had been to many places, had drunk many kinds of water and had taken baths and diet, and still she had received no help. But, at length, persuaded by my healing and the importuning of her sisters, she presented herself to me for treatment. I gave treatment and also a daily explanation of the little I knew of Christian Science, and, at the end of four weeks, she had been "made new," and, in her own words, "I feel as light and happy as a bird," was told the story of the coming of the healing Christ to her consciousness.

Because of this healing the sisters began to study the Bible and the Christian Science text-book, but with many misgivings, as they soon saw that there were many things in both that were at variance with their previous conceptions of God and Christ. Suffice it to say that by diligence on their part and by patience on the part of my wife and myself, they are now in the true fold and are loyal followers of Mrs. Eddy, giving thanks daily for the light that has come into their lives and home.

To reassure those who may have the idea that they need to know all about this Science before they can hope to help themselves or others, I wish to call attention to the fact that this supposedly incurable case was taken up by me about one month after I first began to study Christian Science, and was met and mastered before I had been in Christian Science two months.

The next case that presented itself to me was a case of nervousness, so extreme that it had driven the patient to the very borderland of insanity, and because of the long continuance of the disease, the patient was in the blackest despair, and melancholia was in evidence in its most hopeless form. The conditions and environment surrounding the patient were also of the worst, for he was a saloon-keeper. I had now been studying Christian Science ten weeks, and as I had been successful in overcoming every ill that I had so far attempted to master, my faith in the healing power of Truth was almost absolute, and, consequently, I did not hesitate a moment in the taking of this case, although I was careful to tell the patient that I had only been studying this Science a short time, and that if I failed in helping him he must not blame the Science, but lay the failure to my limited understanding. I also tried to induce this man to have a regular practitioner, but to no avail, as he knew of the healing of my sister-in-law; and, as he had known of her long illness, he said he would have no other practitioner. There was progress made from the very start, but it was not marked, as this man proved to be a veritable "doubting Thomas" and would admit nothing until he was literally forced to do so by his own understanding of the Science. This case was under constant treatment for three months, and because of the very nervous condition of the patient he would come to me personally with questions or complaints as often as three times every day. I studied my text-book every spare moment, and when my patience and confidence were almost exhausted, my Leader's statement in Science and Health—that "Patience must 'have her perfect work' "—would give me renewed confidence and patience. At the end of the first month's treatment much of the fear was conquered, and the patient was beginning to have more hope and to take more interest in the work, as was evidenced by his beginning to read and study the text-book in a calmer frame of mind. I was also becoming more certain of my own ground, and my faith was surely, though slowly, as it seemed to me, changing to understanding. It also became gradually known to a great many of my friends in our city that I had been healed in Christian Science, and that I had taken up the work, and that at that very time I was treating several people. To make my work harder, I was told by various ones that I was not doing right in treating a saloon-keeper. Not yet having landed on the rock of understanding, I was sorely perplexed. To make matters worse, one who, I thought, knew, but with more zeal than understanding, took it upon herself to remonstrate with me about my doings, and, among other things, told me that it would be impossible to heal a saloon-keeper until he had given up his business, and that it was neither Christian nor scientific to try to heal anyone who was in such a business. In proof of her words, she pointed me to the case itself, stating that I had admitted that the case was gaining very slowly. It seemed to me at this time that I stood all alone, with all the world against me; for, as I began to attend the Christian Science Church, my relatives were fearful because I had abandoned the religion of my childhood, and, although not much was said by them to me on the subject of my former religion, yet I could feel that they were opposed to the course I was pursuing. At the time I felt like a lost sheep, but now I am thankful that I was obliged to stand alone, as this very situation compelled me to stick close to my text-book and my Bible. Often, when in doubt, the thought so frequently advanced by Mrs. Eddy, that God is all power, and the only power, would come to my thought, and I would think and mentally declare, "My God is an all-powerful God, and He cares not for condition nor environment, and, being all-powerful, He can heal a saloon-keeper in his saloon or elsewhere." My patient knew nothing of the mental struggle that I was undergoing, neither did I tell him aught of what I had heard regarding the incurability of his case, but I was continually admonishing him to lead the very best life he was capable of living and that I was sure that he would be healed. In justice to this man, I will state that he never drank one drop of intoxicating liquor while under treatment, nor has he since, and it is now five years. At the end of three months' treatment this case was so far met that the patient, at my request, endeavored to stand alone, but, at the end of two weeks, I thought it advisable to again give a few treatments to help him stand, and from that day to this he has needed no more treatment, except such as he was able to give himself. He at once became a regular attendant of the Christian Science Church, and was, and is to-day, one of the most regular attendants that we have, and I do not know of a more conscientious, careful and thankful student of our text-book. Perhaps you would like to know what was said by those friends who kindly but wrongly advised me. To honest hearts this healing was an object lesson of the all-power and all-inclusiveness of God, and they profited greatly by it, but the one that had personally admonished me that I was doing wrong in treating this case took refuge behind a statement that I had healed this man through hypnotism and that it was only a temporary cure, for was not the man still conducting his nefarious business? But even at this early day of my Christian Science experience I had perceived a little of the truth contained in the Master's statement (Matt. 12:27): "If I by Beelzebub cast out devils, by whom do your children cast them out?" So I said to this lady, "I don't believe that Beelzebub can or would cast out Beelzebub;" and she said: "Time will tell how you cast him out"; and I am glad to report that time has told, for the man, of his own volition, has now sold out his saloon and is studying our text-book more diligently than before, with the express purpose of taking class instruction and becoming a Christian Science practitioner. Even to-day his understanding of the Christ, Truth, is such that he has been able to reflect the healing Truth to a marked degree, and I bespeak for him a grand success in his new field of endeavor.

I have described this case and its ultimately successful issue in such detail because there are many who, when they first come to Christian Science, come with such a feeling of self-condemnation, because of their former life, that they are sore afraid and much in doubt as to whether there is healing and salvation for such sinners as they, and to such as these I cannot do better than quote the words of Jesus: "They that are whole need not a physician; but they that are sick. I came not to call the righteous, but sinners to repentance." So I add that, no matter what has gone before, turn yourself, and with the right motive and purpose in your heart and a constant endeavor to act and think correctly, there is healing and saving for you.

Although it was now only five months since I began the study of Christian Science and only four months since I was healed in this Science, I was beginning to have more calls for treatment than I could find time to give. Most of the cases that presented themselves were of the kind that *materia medica* had called incurable; others were such as had undergone operations and had not been helped thereby. To those unfamiliar with Christian Science practice it may seem strange that the majority of the cases that came to me were of this character, but if they will bear in mind that very few people apply for Christian Science healing until after the regular physicians have failed to cure them, my statement will not seem strange. Being still a mere "babe in Christ," I will admit that some of the cases looked very formidable to me, for my thought was still at times somewhat vacillating. First faith, then fear, then hope, and again doubt, would have possession. At such times I would always have recourse to my text-book, and by careful and studious reading of the chapter "Christian Science Practice," I would add a little to my limited understanding, and again gain faith and confidence in the all-power of Mind —God—and would then work the harder to reduce the false appearance named disease to its native nothingness.

It was about this time that a lady came to me for treatment who had, about six months before this, undergone a serious operation and had not received the relief she had hoped for. At the advice of her physician she was ready to undergo a second operation when her attention was called to Christian Science by a friend. This lady did all she could to impress me with the thought that her case was the worst one ever known, and tearfully assured me that her trouble was not a merely imaginary one, but was very real, as she could readily prove, for she had been carefully examined by Dr. ———, a very noted specialist, and he had told her about it himself. This lady, like many other persons that I have met with since, had the idea that perhaps Christian Science might help such cases as were merely imaginary but could do little or nothing for cases that were "real," as she expressed it.

Her tale of trouble was a long one, but, supported by faith in God, I was not daunted thereby, and took the case. At the end of one week all the terribleness and "reality" were gone and the lady told me that the second day after I had started treatment she was well enough to go about her regular work, and there was not even a symptom left; but when I suggested that, this being the case, she would not need any more treatment, she became much alarmed, and begged me to give her attention for at least one more week, for fear that this terrible trouble might come back. I tried to assure her that there was no danger of its coming back, but nothing would satisfy her except that I give her another week's treatment, which I at last consented to do, to allay her fear rather than for any other reason. The trouble never came back, for there wasn't anything to come back.

CHAPTER II

My office was at my home and nearly all the treatments were given there, and my wife saw the sick come and saw them go away healed. For some time she had said nothing to me about my old religion, but she was not yet ready for the new. But the many things that she had heard and seen in connection with my practice were slowly but surely making their impression, as was evidenced by her not asking me to go to the old church; and the time came when I noticed that she had not attended service for several Sundays herself. I made no comment, knowing that deeds speak louder than words.

My wife had had an affliction of the eyes that had caused her to wear specially ground glasses for a number of years, and the oculist had assured her that she would always need to wear them, and even with the glasses in constant use the eyes would frequently inflame to such a degree that she could scarcely bear any light. At such times she would carefully apply the eye-water that the oculist had prepared for such occasions, and this eye-water always seemed to allay the inflammation in the course of a few days, but at length there came a time when the eye-water would not do its accustomed work even when applied twice as often as prescribed. Although my wife did not know why the remedy had failed her, I was sure that I knew why the lotion had seemed to lose its curative properties,—that through all she had heard and seen she had, without clearly recognizing it herself, lost faith in drugs, and as the drug had no healing virtue in itself it could do no healing. The healing that had been accomplished in the previous applications had come from her faith and not from the drug, and, consequently, her faith in the drug having been destroyed, there was no other healing element left, and she received no benefit from the application of the drug. After three days of trouble and continued applications of the eye-water, the morning of the fourth day dawned, and this was the day of the party to which my wife had been invited and to which she had looked forward with happy expectations, but the eyes seemed worse than ever,—in fact, she could not bear to look up because the light hurt them so. After breakfast I was soon busy treating my patients. The eye lotion was on the table in reach of my wife's hand. The applications were now more frequent than the day before, for her eyes must be at least presentable by half-past one, as that was the time set for the party. At nine o'clock the eyes were examined before the mirror and were found worse. Up to this time my wife had not asked me for treatment for anything, but now she came into the room highly indignant, and said, "It's a pity that you would not help me, if you can do anything for me with your Christian Science!" I quietly answered her, saying, "You have never asked me to give you Science treatment." She answered, "You ought to help me without my asking you." I did not reply to this, merely asking, "Will you stop using the eye-water?" She said, "We will use both, for I must get my eyes in a presentable condition by one o'clock." I answered, "No, I will not treat you unless you promise to stop using that medicine." "I won't stop using it," she said. I made no reply, but went on with my regular work. Ten o'clock came and my wife spoke again, this time more kindly, saying, "Will, I will leave off the medicine until to-night, but if I am no better by that time I will start using it again." Honorably I could not make this concession, and I was sure that by evening they would be better; I also wished to conquer this medicine habit then and there, and do it completely; so I said, "No, you must agree not to use the lotion again under any condition." There was a moment's hesitation; then she said, "All right, I will never use it again, but help me if you can"; and she placed the medicine in the medicine cabinet out of sight. I believe I worked that morning as I never worked before to attain to that Mind that was also in Christ Jesus, for

I truly longed to have my dear wife come into the truth that makes free, and I felt that if I was successful in my endeavor to heal her eyes through the application of Truth, this would induce her to become a student of Truth. Very few were the words that passed between us from that time until dinner, when my wife said, "Will, my eyes are much better." I told her to get ready to go to the party, and that I would keep up the treatment. At one-thirty she presented herself before me, saying, with a smiling countenance, "I look quite presentable, don't I? and I can look up without any inconvenience." I assured her that she would be entirely well in a short time and that I would treat her during her absence, which I did, and when she came home at half-past five there was no trace of the recent trouble to be seen. Shortly after, my wife discovered that she could see as well without the glasses as with them and stopped using them, and now, nearly five years later, her sight is better than it ever was before, and she can see to do the finest needle-work without any inconvenience and without the aid of glasses. She has never used the glasses from the day she first took them off.

I now come to an experience that caused me much trouble but which also taught me a wholesome lesson. In speaking with one of my patients to whom I had just started to give treatment, I asked the question, "Have you ever heard of the book, Science and Health, with Key to the Scriptures, by Mary Baker Eddy?" The answer was, "I have a book called Science and Health, but I don't believe that the author's name is Eddy." Having been in Christian Science so short a time, I was not yet aware that there were other books written, the titles to which were very similar to that of the Christian Science text-book. I asked this patient to bring me the book, as I wished to read and compare it with the Science and Health which I owned. So on her next call she brought it, and the title was very similar to "Science and Health." I asked permission to keep the book until I should have the time to give it a thorough reading, which request was granted, and the next day I began to read this book. I noticed that many of the statements were similar to the statements I found in my text-book. Still I detected a difference, but could not analyze this difference at that time. I also noted that there were some printed forms of treatment,—at least, that is what they seemed to my thought, and at first I was pleased that the book had come to my notice. At this time I was treating five or six patients and with good success. Some were being healed more slowly than others, but all reported a steady gain up to the time that I began the reading of the book that she brought, and I myself was very well both physically and mentally. I continued my study of that part of this new book which I, for want of a better name, will call formulas of treatment. Gradually, and almost imperceptibly, this reading changed my former thought, and, of course, as a consequence, my mode of treating my patients changed. In a few days I began to hear complaints from every one of my patients, and I myself noticed a sort of dull pain in the head which hindered me from clear thought. As my patients began to complain I began to work and study the harder, and as this did not seem to bring the desired relief, I began to try the various formulas given, and also to make each treatment of longer duration, but the only result was that I began to have this dull pain in the head constantly, and the more I treated myself the worse the pain seemed to grow. I began to suspect that the book my patient had loaned me was in some way responsible for my trouble, but just why or how this could be possible was a mystery to me, for surely the book seemed full of the word of God, as I found many Bible quotations in it and also the statement that Mind is God, just as I had found in Mrs. Eddy's writings. Then, where was the trouble? I was entirely at a loss, and at length arrived at the conclusion that it must be something else.

In talking matters over with my wife, she made the remark: "You have been well continually since you were healed in Science until you began to study that other book, and I believe that something that you have read in that has led your thought astray." This made me again think that the book which I had read was in some way accountable for my feeling so very ill. I determined to try to work it out myself, but my wife became alarmed at my condition and begged me to allow her to call the practitioner through whose efforts I had been healed, which I at length consented to. When she arrived I explained to her what I had been reading and she said that she had no doubt but that this was the trouble, and began treating me, and, on the advice of my practitioner, I began to read carefully our textbook. By the next morning I was much better, and a day or two later I was again free from the dullness and mental confusion. I now again began the treatment of my patients, and was careful to treat in accordance with the instructions given under the heading "Mental Treatment Illustrated" in Science and Health, by Mrs. Eddy, and again my patients began to report a steady gain. This was so remarkable that I determined to sift the matter to the bottom and find out, if possible, what the difference in the two methods really was, for a difference there must be, as I was just as honest and conscientious in my application of the one method as I was in the other, but the result of one system (Mrs. Eddy's) freed me and my patients from bondage and pain, while the other caused me to suffer and no gain resulted to my patients. I set apart several hours each day to be devoted to thought on this subject, and slowly but surely the light came. The difference in the two methods can be stated in a very few words, but to make clear to the beginner this difference will take many more. I discovered by careful search and thought that in Christian Science as taught by Mrs. Eddy, the divine Mind—God—is the healer, while in the other method much was said about God, and God was also named Mind, and many Scriptural quotations were cited, and Jesus was called the Christ, but when it came to actual practice,—that is, when outlining the method to be used in liberating ourselves and others from ills and troubles,—the mortal thought or mortal mind was the active agent, and, instead of allowing reason and revelation to do their work, this other method used the mortal mind or will force, in the form of suggestion and concentration of thought, and this willing and concentrating of thought, not being correct practice, it brought on a sense of straining, and this willing the patient to be well and straining to make one's thought felt on or by the patient produced its effect on the operator and thus caused him a dullness in the head, and gradually robbed the operator of the power of clear thought, hence the mental confusion that I had experienced. In other words, one is the method of the Christ Mind, overcoming the error in the patient's consciousness, and the other is a semi-hypnotic method, trying, by sheer will-force, to influence the patient's thought and change it regardless of right or wrong. The Christ method demonstrates for the patient the right of dominion and self-government under God, while the other method deprives him still more than the disease has deprived him of dominion and self-government, making him subject to the government of another human will. One is the method of destroying a belief through the application of Truth, and the other is the method of casting out a lesser belief or evil by a greater. Although I had suffered much through my mistake, I felt that the lesson which it taught me was some compensation, as I have ever since been free from this error.

CHAPTER III

My family consists of my wife, myself and a son, now a young man nineteen years of age. This son when less than two years of age was attacked by that dread disease which *materia medica* calls spinal meningitis, and although his life was spared, the physicians assured us that, though he might live and grow up, he would never be mentally bright. We also noticed that the child had become cross-eyed.

True to the predictions of the physicians, the boy's so-called mental power did not develop, and he became a great care to us. He was never vicious, but my wife and I were often humiliated by the boy's actions before other people; and when he began to go to school our troubles multiplied because of the actions of the other children, and as time went on his schoolmates soon outstripped him in his studies, and after more than six years of schooling, and at the time of my coming into Christian Science, he could scarcely add two and two.

When first I came into Christian Science there was so much that needed to be attended to that I seemed to find no time to look after my son's case, for we were in debt and many other things seemed to need my attention first. However, after a few months, I began work on my son's case, and soon he evinced a desire to leave off the glasses that he had found necessary to wear for years. After some persuasion on his part and because he told us he could see better without them, we let him take them off, but the eyes were so badly turned that I was much distressed whenever I chanced to glance at him. But I kept on with the treatments, and soon the eyes began to straighten to a normal position, and a few months later no one could detect from looking at him that at one time his eyes had been crossed, and no trace of it has ever appeared since. Years before this time the boy had undergone two different surgical operations, both of which proved failures. In fact, the eyes seemed worse after the operations, and the sight in one eye was so poor that the boy had always, when attending school, to request the teacher to allow him to sit close to the blackboard, so that he might see what she had written thereon, but now, although my sight has become so keen that, when out in the open with my friends I can nearly always distinguish forms and faces at a greater distance than those who are with me, yet my son's sight excels my own. Although his mental development was not so rapid, yet it was constant, and in many ways he is now as far advanced as the average boy of his age, and his health is almost perfect. In size and strength he is much above the average. All this we owe to the blessed truth made practical, which our Leader has named Christian Science.

During all this time, and through all this healing and growing prosperity, I had never requested my wife to go with me to the Christian Science services; neither had I said anything to oppose her going to her church, feeling that in due time she would see the light and of herself follow it. One Sunday morning she walked up to me, and, tenderly placing her hand on my shoulder, asked, "Will, would you like me to go with you to the Christian Science Church?" I answered, "I don't think you had better go until you are entirely convinced that Christian Science is the truth." A week or two later my wife asked, "Do you think any of the Scientists would object if I were to go to their services?" I said, "No, they will be glad to give you a hearty welcome." She then replied, "Then I am going with you"; and this was said in so determined a voice that I was convinced that she had decided once and for all. I would have liked to have shown the joy that was in my heart, but thought best not to say much at that time. We went that day, and my wife has been a constant attendant ever since, and many times I have heard her say, "I don't see how I could have been so ignorant as to believe many of the things that I did believe in the old thought." We were now happier than ever, and my wife is loyal through and through to the cause of Christian Science, and does much good in spreading the Gospel amongst those that are in trouble and afflicted.

CHAPTER IV

I have three sisters who were all considered staunch supporters of the faith of my childhood, and when I thought of them a yearning would come into my heart to tell them of this new-old religion which was doing so much for me and mine. One of these sisters had been an invalid for years. Her malady was of such a nature that at times the pain almost deprived her of her reason, and there had been a steady decline in strength. Her husband and daughter were often fearful that perhaps the next attack would prove fatal. I knew that in former years this sister had attended church quite regularly, and thought much of her religion, but not to the extent that her thought was narrow; but, with failing health, she, like many others, turned more and more to her church, hoping against hope that, perhaps, in being a good attendant at church and following as closely to its teachings as she could, God would be more apt to hear her prayers and give her relief from this hell of pain. To such an extent did she carry her devotion that she rarely missed a service, but still she continued to grow worse. I was perplexed as to what method I had better use in bringing the *good news* to her. I had already written her that I had been healed, and through what means the healing had been accomplished. Like many others, I had supposed that all that I had to do was to tell my brothers and sisters of the wonderful healing which I had experienced, and they would be more than ready to try the same method, but my letter merely brought an acknowledgment of its having been received and that they were all exceedingly glad of my recovery, etc., but nothing further. After some time I decided to pay this sister a personal visit and let her see how well I was looking, and perhaps this would make an opening. I arrived at my sister's home on an early evening train, and I found that their only daughter, a young woman of twenty, was ill. After the customary greetings had been exchanged, I inquired as to what the trouble was, and was told that the daughter had been having a severe attack of nausea, and that it had been more or less in evidence for weeks, and that nothing they had tried had availed to stop it. It seemed to me, almost, that this opportunity to demonstrate the power of Truth over error had been made especially for this occasion, and, in conformity with this thought, I gradually led the conversation in the direction of my own healing and of the method used to heal me. I also told of a number of cases that I had been instrumental in bringing out of bondage through the Christ, Truth, and told them something of Mind's government of the body, being careful not to give offense.

There happened to be standing on a table near by a small dish of salted peanuts, and in my desire to make plain the fact that material things of themselves have no power, I referred to the peanuts in this manner: "Some people have the belief that if they eat peanuts they will be distressed, but peanuts, not possessing any life or action of their own, cannot in reality have a distressing effect on anyone. The ill effect comes because of the belief or wrong thought of those who are distressed." The daughter spoke up at once and said: "That sounds very reasonable to me, and as I have had a craving for those very peanuts for several days I am going to eat them." But the mother at once interposed with objections, reminding the daughter that the last time she ate them she had been sick all night. The daughter appealed to me, and I said: "If you are not afraid that they will harm you, and keep fear out of your thought, you will experience no trouble, but if you do decide to eat them, I wish you would let me treat you so as to make doubly sure. Besides, there is no need of your suffering with this false sense of nausea, and when I treat you I will try to free you from this trouble." Her answer was, "All right, I'll eat, if you will treat." The mother looked anxious, but I assured her as best I could, and cited her a few cases that were of a similar nature. The daughter ate the peanuts and I treated her. In less than half an hour she was sitting up and was as jolly as the rest of us. The next morning there was no appearance of the trouble, and the case was entirely healed. This little demonstration did much to influence my sister to try the same method of healing for herself, but progress was very slow, because she was not yet ready to let go of her former views, and everything that was not in accord with her religion was usually criticized; and many things that she read antagonized her to such an extent that she would stop all study and treatment, only to take it up again a little later. Suffice it to say that now this sister is an ardent student of our text-book, and with renewed health and vigor she is following the Christ as shown to her in Science and Health. The daughter's progress in understanding was much faster, and for the last two years she has been able to take care of herself and also help others.

In the beginning, while this sister's thought was swinging back and forth between faith and doubt, hope and despair, she wrote a letter to our sister who resided in a small city in Missouri, telling her of my healing and of my leaving the faith of our father and mother, and that I had been to see her and had advised her to look into this new religion, as she called it. This brought a letter of censure and admonition to me from the sister in Missouri. Among other things, she said that I should at once turn back to my former religion if I did not wish to lose my soul, and with much sincerity pointed out to me that if I persisted in my present course, there could be only one result,—that at death I would be sentenced to hell to suffer eternally. This threat had often been thundered at me in my childhood, and perhaps had much to do with my attendance at church as a child, but as I grew to manhood this threat lost much of its force, and now as I read it in my sister's letter it merely brought a smile; for even the little understanding that I had acquired of God had liberated me from the belief of a place called hell and also from the thought of eternal damnation. I thought carefully for several days, and then wrote this sister a long and loving letter, and in the letter made many references to the Bible. This I did with the purpose that she should be compelled to look them up in the Bible, and through this search I felt that she would see somewhat of Truth. I knew that she, like others of this denomination, had never read much in the Bible, but had taken for granted, through blind faith, all that had been preached to her as absolute truth. My letter awakened her to such an extent that she was worried, and she carried my letter to her pastor, and in response I got a letter in which was cited many Bible quotations which on their face seemed to uphold her church, but they were the same that I had heard from childhood, and I had long since, for my own information, studied them until I had arrived at their true meaning, and now the letter that she supposed would be final, and would convince me of the error of my ways, was the thing that I needed to conclusively prove to her the fallacy of her present views. I wrote to her, commenting on all of the Bible citations in her letter in the light which I had obtained from Christian Science, but did no urging, merely telling her that I left the entire matter to her own judgment.

For a long time no answer came, but finally I received a letter, which stated that she had been all this time studying the Bible by herself, and from the viewpoint that I had explained, with the result that she was sure that Christian Science was right, and she asked me for reading matter pertaining to this Science. I sent some at once and also advised the purchase of Science and Health, and told her where in her city she could buy it. This sister's understanding of Christian Science has now developed to the point where she is able to demonstrate over whatever ills may afflict herself and her children, and she has also been able to reflect Truth for the healing of others not in the family. At present she is studying with renewed zeal to prepare herself to become a regular practitioner of Christian Science.

All this careful study and seeking for reasonable explanation did much to unfold my thought, and I could see that gradually my consciousness was expanding and rising higher out of matter, and a temporal view of things, into Spirit, the realm of the real and eternal; that is, I was slowly but surely sifting the wheat from the chaff, former beliefs were being cast out by understanding, and the Truth that I was comprehending was surely setting me free from my former bondage, just as Jesus said that Truth would do. At this point of my progress from sense to Soul, from things perceived materially to things known spiritually, I thought that I had lost all sense of God as a person sitting on a throne in a place called heaven, but an incident now happened that proved to me that I had not yet entirely freed myself of this former belief. Through thinking of God as Mind, everywhere present, I had, as it were, mentally spread my thought of this one-time personal God over all creation, yet there was a sense of form, even though it was very indistinct. But an event transpired that destroyed this newer illusion. A lady whom I knew very well and whom I considered a most honest and devout Christian, presented herself to me for treatment. I esteemed this lady so highly that I considered her a very much better person and Christian than myself, and after she had stated her troubles to me, questions arose in my mind. Why should this good woman be suffering? Had she prayed to God for relief? Her answer was, "Yes, many, many times." My next thought was, "Why had God not heard her prayers and healed her? Would He hear my prayers and heal her?" Yes, I was positive of that. Then this thought came: Here is a woman who, without doubt, is much better than I am, and she has asked and asked and has not received. It seemed to me as though a very righteous person had presented herself for healing through the prayers of one less good. No doubt entered my mind that she would be healed, and she was healed very quickly. Why did not God answer the prayer of this good woman? It was not because He did not wish her to be healed, for she was now well and had been healed in answer to prayer. Did she not know how to pray aright? Perhaps this was the trouble; but wherein was the woman's mistake? She had surely prayed with an honest heart and, no doubt, with all the faith that she was capable of mustering. Why had not my prayers in former days been answered? Ah, here was the solution! Why had I not seen it before? This woman, like myself before I came into Christian Science, had been praying to a personal God to heal her; in other words, she had been pleading with a mental image, a creation of her own imagination, a much magnified human personality, to heal her, and as this mental image had no real existence, it necessarily was a myth of her own creation with neither intelligence nor power. When next I met this lady I asked her to describe to me her conception of God, and it was much as I had thought.

Seeing clearly now why her prayers had not been answered, I asked myself the question, Do I also see clearly why my prayer was answered, and wherein the prayers differed, for there must be a difference, as was clearly shown by the results. In looking for the solution I mentally pictured forth three forms, one to represent the woman, the other myself, and the third, God. I imagined one of these forms at each point of a triangle. Now I imagined the woman pleading with God, and I at once saw why her prayer had not been answered,—simply because this humanized God was a myth and had no existence or power. I again arranged this mental triangle and asked myself the question, Did I also plead with this mythical third party that was supposed to be at one of the angles? And the answer I had to make to myself was, that, in a slight degree, I had also pleaded with this mythical conception, only my conception was not that of a form, for, as previously stated, my thought of a personal God had been spread all over the universe, because I perceived Him as everywhere present. I saw at once that, in so far as I had pleaded with this false sense of God, my effort had been lost, but still I must have prayed aright at least partially, or the lady would not have regained her health so quickly. For several days I tried to arrive at a conclusion which would satisfy my reason, but could not. I then took my concordance to Science and Health and read every statement in the book wherein the word God appeared, and in this way received the light I was looking for. Slowly but surely I began to understand that God is Principle and not person, and that Truth is Principle. At once it was apparent to me wherein my prayer had differed from the lady's prayer. Her thought or prayer was that she was sick, and that perhaps God was responsible for the sickness, whereas my prayer or thought had been in conformity with Principle, Truth, which is, that, God being perfect and the only cause, the manifestation must be the forever perfect image and likeness of this perfect cause; hence her sickness was not real, or a real condition, but was the manifestation of a false belief, and, not being real but only a mental misconception, it was destructible through the application of the Truth of Being, which Truth I had partially become conscious of when treating the lady and had reflected it to her.

I now found myself on a surer footing and my healing work was correspondingly quicker and better. I do not wish it understood that all the healing that had been accomplished through my efforts up to this time was done without any understanding, but I fully recognize the fact that, up to this time, there was perhaps more faith than understanding, while now faith was based on understanding, or faith had become understanding.

CHAPTER V

My intention, when I started this book was to write of every case that had come to me for treatment, but I had not written far when I found it necessary to refresh my memory by looking at my reference files, and then I became aware of the fact that if I carried out my thought of writing of every case, this book would need to be several times the customary size; so I have been taking only such cases as I thought would be of especial interest.

Up to this time there had been presented to me and healed by Truth, cases of melancholy, nervous prostration, mental disturbance bordering on insanity, heart trouble, stomach troubles, female troubles, cross-eyes, impaired sight, tuberculosis of the bowels, rheumatism, arthritis deformans, dyspepsia, la grippe, liver complaint, and the many minor things, like neuralgia, headache and toothache. Nearly all of these cases had been pronounced incurable, or had not been benefitted by the regular medical practitioners, and the names above given to the various cases were given by these medical practitioners after careful diagnosis.

I will now write of a case of arthritis deformans. The patient was a young man of about twenty-two years of age. His fingers, hands, and arms were so deformed that he was practically helpless, not being able to move himself without aid. He had to be dressed and undressed, and needed assistance when taking food; in fact, it was with great difficulty that he managed even to hold a spoon in his hand. I began treatment and soon there were signs of improvement, but not as rapidly as I expected, and upon investigation I found that the patient was not following my instructions; and, to make matters worse, some of his relatives were opposed to his being treated in Science, and would tell him that he was very foolish to throw his money away in such a manner, and that, if they were he, they would go back to the old family doctor or engage a specialist. But the young man had had the first relief for months from incessant pain when I began to treat him. Therefore he decided to continue treatment with me, but, of course, all this adverse talk and criticism seemed to have weight and made him much discouraged. Being in another city, I could not see him very often, but nevertheless he was surely being healed, as was evidenced by a return of strength, and by the fact that he became able to take care of himself and could dress and undress himself. A little later he was able with the aid of a cane to walk about the house, and one day ventured to walk down to the business portion of his city, a place he had not been for months. I had warned him not to tell anyone of the treatment he was taking, but in his great enthusiasm at being again able to walk and take care of himself, he became unwise, and on that day of his first visit to town he told everyone that asked him about his recovery that he was taking Christian Science treatment and gave the credit to this treatment. At once he became the target of ridicule and adverse prophecy. One would laugh at him, while the next would tell him that he would not stay healed, and that soon he would be worse than ever, and yet others would tell him that they had seen other people hypnotized and that no doubt he would wake up in a few days in a worse condition than when he commenced treatment, and minus his money. The next letter that I received did not contain the customary news that the gain was constant and that he was rapidly coming into perfect health, but on the contrary, that he was not so well as usual, and there also seemed a sense of censure in the letter. I supposed that perhaps this change was just a little return of former conditions brought on by allowing his thought to dwell on the past; so I wrote a very encouraging letter, pointing out all that had already been accomplished, and exhorting him to have faith and to expect a complete and speedy cure. But the next letter brought worse news than the previous one; in fact, it was full of misgivings, and expressed the thought that all his troubles were returning, and if there was not soon a change for the better, he would again try his old family doctor, but not a word about his having been down town and having met the ridicule of the wiseacres of the town was given. I at once decided that there must have been a cause for this sudden change and I took the next train, to find out just what it all meant. By answers to my questions I was soon made aware of the trouble, and by illustration and explanation I showed the young man the cause of his present condition, and also his lack of wisdom in not following the advice I had given him. After three weeks of almost constant work I again got this case on the highroad to health, and the patient himself began to do all that he could to help himself, and he was healed, whereas he was a helpless, hopeless sufferer before Christian Science came into his life. He is now a healthy, happy, and prosperous member of his community. In handling this case I again learned a useful lesson, and although the conditions that I had met gave me much extra work to do, I felt that the experience was worth the work. I now saw the probable reason why Jesus told some of those whom he healed to "go and tell no man." It was probably because he understood the baneful effect of adverse and discouraging thought on those who knew not how to destroy the seeming power of mortal mind. I do not wish it understood that these people who said discouraging things to my patient did so from any sinister or malicious motives,—far from it, for many who said these things were close friends of this young man and wished him only the best of everything; but it was all done through ignorance, and because mortals, as a rule, like to be thought wiser than they are.

As the month of October came of this, my first year in Christian Science, my thought went back to the October of the previous year. I could hardly realize the change that had been wrought in my life. For a moment my thought returned to contemplate the old condition, and this is what I saw,—myself almost too weak to stand on my feet, sick in body and mind, slowly and with painful effort trying to walk down town to the doctor's office, about seven blocks away, feeling too poor in purse to spend the five cents that would have carried me on the street-car. I mentally saw the old, low, stone wall about half-way, on which I was compelled to rest before I could proceed farther, then another long rest before I dared to venture to climb the stairs that led to the doctor's office, the half-hour's wait in the anteroom, and then I was in the presence of the doctor. His friendly and customary "Well, how are you to-day?" and my customary and doleful "I am no better," came clearly to recollection. Then as I continue my contemplation I hear myself saying, "Doctor, I have come to-day to know the worst. Is there no hope for me?" Then the doctor's reply, given with a brave attempt at a smile, "You know the old saying, that while there's life there's hope." I can see myself insisting to know the worst, and I also notice the smile on his kindly face change to a look of seriousness, and at length he slowly answers: "Mr. Walter, since you insist, I will give you a little advice. If you have any affairs or papers to get in shape, do it at once, as I don't think you will be with us by Christmas."

I had heard the worst, my death sentence as it were, and thanked the doctor for telling me. It was only what I had expected. Christmas came, also the first of the year, and although I had not passed out of this earthly sense of existence, I was fully aware that the time was surely drawing nigh. January came and passed, then came February, with me looking daily for the "grim reaper," and then, thank God, came February 12th, the opening of the book, and the angel of God's presence, Christian Science, with healing in its wings. Am I thankful? Suffice it to say that I fully realize that had not Jesus taught the disciples, and had not Mrs. Eddy written "Science and Health," my wife would to-day be a widow and my son fatherless. Am I thankful? I have tried to prove by my works that I am. I have given my life to the work of Christian Science and to the promulgation of its text-book, "Science and Health with Key to the Scriptures," by Mary Baker Eddy.

Now I come to the time of my first Christmas in Christian Science. I do not like to look back into the old life, but I cannot help comparing the last Christmas in the old life with this first Christmas in Christian Science. In viewing that last Christmas I can remember nothing but sickness, pain, feebleness, sorrow, and poverty, while on this first Christmas in Christian Science I see nothing but peace, joy, health, happiness, and plenty for every member of my family. To those who have not experienced the healing Christ, this change may seem an exaggeration, but I have not told the half. The mental freedom, the spiritual uplift, the cessation from fear, worry and doubt, were much the greater blessings. Enough of retrospection. Let the past bury the past, with its hideous nightmare of the dreams of darkness.

Shortly after this first Christmas in the new life a friend came to see me for the express purpose of finding out whether it was really true that I had been healed through Christian Science and that I had left my former belief and embraced Christian Science. I told her of my healing and of the many good things that had come to me. This friend could hardly believe the witness of her eyes regarding the change in my physical condition as well as my circumstances, and at length she said, "If Christian Science has done all this for you, why cannot I have some of this good?" I assured her that this same good is for all, and her answer was, "Then I want it, and I want you to tell me how to go about it to get it." The result of our conversation was that this lady bought "Science and Health" at once, and became an earnest seeker after Truth, and to-day she is a member of the Mother Church, and of the local Christian Science Society. Her husband also took up the study and he is a member of the Mother Church and a member of the local Christian Science Society, and has been through class and has made many good demonstrations of healing.

I think it was about a month after the lady referred to above had become interested in Christian Science that she came to me one day and said: "I cannot seem to understand the unreality of evil. I have had a claim of stomach trouble for some time, and I tell you, Mr. Walter, there is no unreality about it. The fact is, it is only too real, and how you people can call a stomachache unreal is more than I can understand."

I could not entirely hide the smile that came to my lips, as it was not so many months ago that I had been in this same mental position myself. I did the best I could to show her the unreality of all error, but the evidence of the aching stomach seemed to weigh more to her physical senses than all that I could say to the contrary. After she had gone home, I carefully took up our conversation, to discover if possible wherein I had fallen short in making the unreality of evil plain to her, and it was while thinking of this that the thought that Jesus had used parables to point out the Truth of Being to his disciples came to my mind, and I decided that I would try to think of a parable that might help this lady see the light. The result of my thought I wrote on a piece of paper, and when next I saw her I handed her the paper. She read it carefully and it seemed to be just what she needed, and the result of her enlightenment was that the stomach trouble was healed. In talking over the incident, this lady urged me to write more along the same line, as the little that I had written had been of such benefit to her. The result was that I decided to write a story book, and later on my first book, entitled "The Pastor's Son," was written and published. In this book is a chapter entitled "The Unreality of Evil," which was the title that I gave the little parable that I gave to this friend and which helped her out of her seeming trouble.

Having been a man known to a great majority of the business people in my home town (I was a salesman and buyer in one of the largest retail establishments in Aurora) and having been sick so long, I thought, when I was healed through Christian Science, that the whole city would turn to this same Science, but I was mistaken. My being healed and my taking up the study of this Science caused hardly a ripple of surprise. Some said, when they heard through what method I had been healed, that I was not nearly as sick as I had pretended to be, while others said, "You can readily see that Mr. Walter only imagined he was sick; for he is now following this new cult which proves conclusively that his mind is affected, so that he might readily have believed that he was ill." But as time wore on and no disposition was shown to commit me to an insane asylum, while, on the contrary, I began to heal cases by the Christ method that our regular physicians had failed to heal, and as reports of my release from poverty began to get abroad, the thought changed, and, whereas I was first accused of being mentally weak, I was now called a shrewd grafter. But these reports disturbed me not at all, for I called to mind an incident of my boyhood days and at once saw that these accusations were of the same nature. I will relate the incident.

I came home from school one day and told my father that one of the boys had accused me of cheating, and that this was the reason that I was at the head of the class. My father answered, "Never mind what the boys say. You keep on 'sawing wood' and you will stay at the head of the class; but if you spend your time wrangling with the other boys you will not have the time to study, and soon you will be at the foot of the class." I thought this good advice at the time, and I decided to follow like good counsel in this instance. My continued success in the healing work also brought me the ill will of a few whom I thought to be true friends, and

I began to hear reports that I was a hypnotist and that the healing that I was accomplishing was being done through hypnotism. This accusation was doubly false,—false, first, because hypnotism does not heal, and second, because the method whereby I was healing was the exact opposite; for hypnotism robs the patient of self-reliance and self-government, while Christian Science teaches self-reliance under God and man's true government by divine Mind. A further proof that I was not healing through hypnotic suggestion was clearly shown by the fact that the people who took treatment from me stayed healed, and a large proportion of them have been able to take care of all their petty ills and also to heal others.

Nearly a year later my book was on sale and met with a hearty welcome, and hundreds of letters of appreciation came to me. Occasionally there came an adverse criticism, pointing to some special statement, and occasionally the statement would be one that many others had found especially interesting or helpful.

Some of the criticisms that came were written in a kindly spirit, were found helpful, and were profited by in later editions of the book. Criticism offered in a helpful spirit is always most welcome to me. Many times my Leader's words, "Each successive stage of experience unfolds new views of divine goodness and love", (Science and Health, page 66, line 14) have been proven true to me.

I soon found that Jesus' statement, "A prophet is not without honor, save in his own country," was being proven true in my own case, for my book was severely criticised by certain people in Aurora, where I live, and I accidentally learned of a number of persons who had been advised not to read the book. Then, from some source word was sent broadcast that the author of "The Pastor's Son" was a non-Scientist and had written the book merely to make money out of Scientists, and reports of this and similar stories began to come back to me by letter from various parts of the country. It ought to have been apparent to any student of Christian Science that a non-Scientist could not write a book containing the matter that is contained in "The Pastor's Son," no matter how much he might wish to. At length the accusation changed form a little, and I began to hear that I was a divinity student, and that I was using the money from the sale of my book to complete my education for entering the ministry. These accusations came to me not merely once or twice,—if that were all I should not mention them here,—but they came to me from all over the land from the Atlantic to the Pacific, and as soon as one of these false stories was met and died out another was forthcoming; and some of them are still in circulation in some parts of the country.

A few months later an incident occurred which gave Madam Gossip new fuel to add to her fire. Having had class instruction, I had my name listed as a practitioner in the Christian Science Journal, not that I was wanting more patients, as I already had many more applying to me for treatment than I could take care of, but because I thought it my duty. After a short time my attention was called to the fact that there was a by-law in the Mother Church Manual to the effect that all those who were listed as practitioners were not to engage in any other business. I at once wrote full particulars to headquarters at Boston regarding the fact that I published my own books and whether this would disqualify me from being listed as a practitioner in the Journal, and I was informed that this did disqualify me, and they advised me to instruct the Publishing Society at Boston to withdraw my name from the list of practitioners, which I did at once. I should here state that there is no by-law or rule to prevent any person from healing the sick whenever and wherever he may have opportunity, no matter what his business; but it is provided that those who are listed in the Journal must give their whole time to that work.

After a while my name was missed from the list in the Journal and at once the news spread through gossip's telephone, and the tale grew until I began to hear from the four quarters of the United States that I was a disloyal student of Mrs. Eddy's, and that on that account my name had been withdrawn from the list of practitioners, all of which, of course was utterly untrue. Still, with all this opposition and false accusation, "The Pastor's Son" won its way, as has also my second book, "The Doctor's Daughter," and they won their way on their merits,—not because of extensive advertising, but because of the friends the books themselves made.

Although I have had much blessed fruit to crown my efforts in Christian Science, I have found that I must also bear the cross. How often have I thought of the words of Mrs. Eddy, given on pages 33 and 34 of "Science and Health": "Have you shared the blood of the New Covenant, the persecutions which attend a new and higher understanding of God? If not, can you then say that you have commemorated Jesus in his cup? If all who seek his commemoration through material symbols will take up the cross, heal the sick, cast out evils, and preach Christ, or Truth, to the poor,—the receptive thought,—they will bring in the millenium." And these words have been an immeasurable comfort to me. Through all this mental stoning I never stopped to wrangle, but kept on working, frequently till daylight would appear, alternately treating my patients and seeking more power, more Truth, from the illumining pages of Mrs. Eddy's various books, and I have never yet looked to them in vain. Often my heart would overflow with sympathy when I thought of the persecution she had undergone, and I knew my persecution was insignificant compared to hers; then at other times I would be almost overwhelmed with the strength and depth of my gratitude to her for having stood firm and thereby made known to mankind the true way to salvation. Why should I not be grateful, for do I not owe my present sense of Life and health to her ceaseless efforts? Was I not lifted from a very hell on earth to a knowledge of the true God and of all the good that this knowledge brings with it, through her works?

"The Pastor's Son" was not written until my second year in Christian Science, but I have found it necessary to speak of it in connection with the incident of the parable of "The Unreality of Evil."

I will now step a few months past the time of my first year in Christian Science, although there is yet much healing that could be told that took place in that first year; but, not wishing to make this book cumbersome, I must drop out some of the good news.

To show that Christian Science is of use every day and in every good way, I will now relate a trip to Arizona taken by a friend and myself, both having some mining interests in that state that we wished to investigate. This friend was not at that time in Christian Science, but knew much of what it had done for me, and was becoming very much interested.

The day of our departure had been set and our tickets and berths had been engaged. It was early spring and the days were still raw and blustery. On the evening of our departure I met my friend and his wife at the depot; the former was suffering from a severe cough and cold, and the latter a little fearful of seeing her husband start on so long a journey under these conditions. A short time before the train was due she remarked to him: "If I were you, I would put off this trip for a few days, until you are rid of this cold." Before I could make any reply my wife, who was standing beside me, said: "Don't worry about that cold; it won't last long when Will gets after it." I then smilingly told the lady that I would see to the cold, and we boarded the train.

That evening I talked a little about Christian Science to my friened, and he signified his willingness that I should treat him for the cough and cold, which I did that same evening.

We arrived in Kansas City the next morning, and found that we had several hours to wait for our connecting train, and decided that we would go up to the business portion of the city. Stepping to the depot door, my friend opened it, to find that a drizzling rain was falling, and he came back and said, "I don't believe I had better go out in that rain with this cough."

We had been up and around for several hours, and I had noticed that my friend had made no attempt to cough, so I said, "I think that cough is gone, for you haven't coughed since we awoke this morning." He looked at me queerly for a moment, then smiled and said, "I guess you are right. I haven't thought of that cough or cold since I went to sleep last night, and if you think it will not harm me, I am ready to go out in this rain." We were out in the drizzling rain more or less for the next three hours, but there was no return of the trouble.

The same evening, as we were getting ready for lunch, I was sitting in my seat with my grip open beside me, when my friend said, "Please hand me my grip; I want to take something out of it." The grip was under my seat, and rather unhandy to get at, so I asked, "What is it that you want? Perhaps I have the same here in mine." He smiled and said, "No, I don't think you carry with you what I am seeking." After a moment he added, "I have been bothered with constipation for years, and find it necessary frequently to take a pill in the evening, to insure a movement of the bowels, and I have noticed that riding on a train aggravates the constipation, so I always carry a bottle of pills with me whenever I take a long trip; I have a full bottle of them in my grip, and that is what I am after."

I told him that if he would leave the pills where they were and not take them I would treat him for the trouble, to which he agreed at once. Upon his return home, three weeks later, he presented his wife with the full bottle of pills, telling her that he had no more use for them. His bowels had not failed to move daily from the time that I started treatment.

My friend was fast coming to have unbounded

faith in Christian Science, and it happened that the next afternoon, as he was passing down the aisle of the car, an old gentleman addressed him and said, "Friend, have you a drop of bitters or liquor with you on the train? I have eaten something that is distressing me terribly." My friend sat down beside the old gentleman and told him that he always carried a bottle of brandy with him on long trips, for medicinal purposes, and that he was welcome to a drink if he wanted it. The old gentleman told him that he did not like liquor of any kind, but that he had no remedy with him, and so had thought of the bitters. My friend then told him that if he did not want the liquor just for the liquor's sake, but merely as a remedy, he would tell him of a better one. The old gentleman assured him that he only wished to get relief from his pain. My friend then told him of his experience with the cold, and said if he were willing, he would ask his friend (meaning me) to help him. The old gentleman again assured him that all he wanted was relief and was willing that I should help him if I were able and so inclined.

I had heard none of the conversation and knew nothing of what had been said, until my friend came to my seat and told me of his conversation. The old gentleman was sitting two seats in front of me, and from his uneasy actions I judged that he was in severe pain, so I told my friend to tell him I would help him, and at once began to treat him. About ten or fifteen minutes later I chanced to look in his direction, and he was just glancing back over the top of his seat at me, and when he saw me he smiled and bowed his head toward me. A few minutes later my friend informed me that the old gentleman was much relieved, and wished to thank me. A half hour later I sat beside him and he said that all the pain was gone. I then told him a little of what Christian Science had done for me and also told him of our text-book, Science and Health.

The next morning after the above incident, our third on the train, I arose about half past seven, and as I entered the toilet room I noticed a young man of perhaps twenty-one years of age, leaning over the lavatory, with blood dripping from his nose into the bowl. I asked him the cause of his trouble and he told me that every time that he got into a high altitude his nose would bleed, and that he had been standing there since four o'clock that morning, and that he was becoming weak from the loss of blood.

I asked him whether he had used any means to stop it, and he told me he had tried everything that had been suggested to him, and then in a very disgusted tone mentioned some of the things he had tried. Here they are: A cold wet towel applied to the base of the brain; a piece of ice held to the forehead; a cold piece of metal—a key in his case—let down along the spine; a silver quarter held under the tongue; a piece of heavy cardboard placed between the teeth and the upper lip and pressed upward tightly. I think there were one or two more remedies, but I have forgotten them.

I was amused while he was doling out his sorrowful experience, but, concealing my amusement, I asked, "Do you want to have that nosebleed stopped?" He informed me very emphatically that he did. I then said, "I will stop it for you if you will do just as I tell you to do." He answered, "I am ready for anything."

The wash-bowl and stand were all spattered with blood, and I thought for a moment how best to get his thought away from all this blood; then said, "I want you to take your handkerchief and hold it to your nose and look out of the car window and carefully observe the scenery that we are passing, and I want you to take special note of it so that you will be able to tell me just what we have passed by, and do not look around until I tell you."

I treated him for perhaps two or three minutes and was conscious that a cure had been effected; then I said, "You may look this way now." He did so, and I said, "Your nose has stopped bleeding; you may now take down the handkerchief."

He did not do so. A look of deep disgust spread over his face, as he said, "I did not think you would make sport of a sick man, and I want you to understand that this is no joking matter, for I am so weak from the loss of blood that I can hardly stand."

I assured the young man that I was not joking, and that if he would only remove the handkerchief from his face he would see that the nosebleed had ceased. It took me longer to convince him that I was not joking, and that the bleeding had really stopped, than it did to make the realization of Truth, by which he had been healed, and finally, when he did take down the handkerchief, he arose and leaned far over the wash-bowl, expecting, of course, that the blood would still be dropping from his nostrils, but when he removed the handkerchief and no blood came, he looked at me in silence, and began to wash the stain from his face and hands and from off the wash-stand.

I silently observed that he was thinking deeply. At length, after he had finished, he turned toward me and with a smile on his face, said, "That's the best trick I ever saw done. Please tell me how you did it."

I spent some time telling him of the wonders of Christian Science, and he went away with the name of our text-book written on a card in his pocket, and also the information just where he could buy one.

The next day we arrived at another point in our journey, where we were obliged to change cars. It was Ash Forks, Arizona. Upon inquiry, finding that we again had several hours to wait for our connecting train, I at once sought out a quiet corner of the palatial depot, where I might read undisturbed, and also enter into my mental closet and be alone with my God if I desired.

My friend, being a railroad man, spent his time watching the arrival and departure of the various trains, for he was much interested in his chosen profession.

We had been waiting, perhaps, a half or three-quarters of an hour, when my traveling companion came to me and said that the trainmen had, a few minutes previously, taken from the train a lady who was in a dangerous condition, the claim being one of high altitude, which was manifested by great distress in breathing and much weakness. He further informed me that he had had a few minutes' conversation with her, and had told her that he had a traveling companion with him that would soon give her ease if she were willing to try his method. When told that the method to be employed was Christian Science, she made no objection, and my friend had come to see if I would again be the good Samaritan. His faith in my efforts were inspiring, to say the least, and I consented to see the lady and treat her if she wished it, which I subsequently did, and she was benefited at once. A short time later, our train arrived and we left her with a smile of thanks on her lips, she having previously asked me for my card, which I gave to her.

Just what the actual results of my treatment were, I did not learn until three years later, when the following letter was received by me, and as it is self-explanatory, I can not do better than give you such parts of it as pertain to the above subject:

Wm. W. Walter,
Aurora, Ill.

Dear Friend,

You will, no doubt, be surprised to receive a letter from me, after a silence lasting three years.

You will remember who I am when I tell you that I am the lady that was taken from a train suffering with the high altitude and asthma, at Ash Forks, Ariz. I was sick almost to death that day, when your friend gave me hope by telling me of you and Christian Science.

The result of your talk and treatment was that all my ills vanished, and the next morning I, in company with my husband and daughter, enjoyed a very hearty breakfast, and I seemed entirely restored to health.

You will remember that in parting you handed

me your card, but told me nothing further of yourself.

* * * Imagine the surprise that came to me, while looking for "The Pastor's Son" in a circulating library, to see your name as the author, and from Aurora, Ill. I walked out of that place with a sense of great pleasure, and humbled by the thought that you had not revealed your identity to me when we parted. I am grateful to God for allowing me the privilege of meeting the author of "The Pastor's Son," who proved himself a true follower of Christ.

Thanking you, I remain,

Yours sincerely,

————.

But let us return to our journey. That night we arrived at our railroad destination, and after a good night's rest we were driven thirty miles across the hot Arizona desert to the edge of the foot-hills where the mining property in which we were interested was situated. Nothing out of the ordinary transpired during the first few days of our stay in the mining camp, but on the third or fourth day an incident occurred that enabled me again to demonstrate the power of Truth over error.

My friend and I had taken with us a camera, as we wished to take some photographic views of the mine, its surroundings, and the work already accomplished, and with the intention of taking some underground photographs we had with us a number of what are known to photographers as flashlight cartridges, which, when lighted, throw out for an instant a very intense, white light.

My friend and myself, with the superintendent of the mine, had gone down one of the shafts for the purpose of taking some flashlight views, and it was while we were engaged in taking these views that the superintendent, in the act of steadying the instrument, placed his hand so close to the flashlight cartridge that when it was lighted it burned his hand so badly that, when viewed in the daylight a few moments later, two of the fingers seemed to be literally cooked, and the back of the entire hand was badly burned.

On leaving camp that morning we had planned on making a general inspection of the shafts and also of all of the various mining claims belonging to the company, but as soon as the superintendent saw the condition of his hand, he at once suggested that we return to camp so that he might give it the attention that he thought necessary. He continued to critically examine his hand, and as I noticed him doing this, I took a handkerchief out of my pocket and tied it loosely about the injured member, but he was insistent that we return to camp.

It was at this time that my friend said, "Mr. ——,"—(calling the superintendent by name)—"you do just as Mr. Walter directs, and you will soon be all right." He then asked me what he was to do, and I advised that we continue our inspection of the property, and that I would take care of the hand.

The next mining claim was perhaps twenty

minutes' walk from where we then were, and I suggested that my friend walk with the superintendent, and that I would follow a little in the rear, not wishing to be disturbed by their conversation. On the way my friend told him of some of the things that he had seen accomplished through my understanding of Christian Science, and this, no doubt, did much good, and by the time we arrived at our destination the gentleman told me that all the pain and burning sensation had ceased, and that he wished to look at the hand. I told him he must not take off the handkerchief, and he obeyed.

Later in the day, when we arrived in camp, the superintendent told some of the miners of the mishap, and how terribly he was burned, and they at once expressed a desire to see the hand, but I told them to wait until the next morning. The superintendent then expressed a wish to remove the handkerchief so that he could wash the burned powder out of the wound, but I advised him to leave it just as it was.

It was long after midnight before I was fully satisfied with my work, and went to sleep. The next morning as I arose and came out of my tent the superintendent was waiting to get my sanction to a removal of the handkerchief; I consented, and when it was removed, all the dirt and burned powder that had been in the wound came off with it, having adhered to the handkerchief. At once all wished to see his hand, and there was a general laugh at his expense for having made such a fuss over a little burn, for all that was left of that burn was a place scarcely half an inch long, where the skin of one finger had cracked open because of the intensity of the heat; all inflammation and soreness was gone, and all that was visible to the eye was a little pink color surrounding the place where the skin had cracked open.

The wonderment of the superintendent was very great; in fact, he said he could hardly credit the evidence of his own eyes.

There was not much inspection of the mining

property that day, as nothing would satisfy the superintendent but that I tell him more and more of this wonderful Science, and that very day he placed three dollars in my hand and made me promise that I would send him a Science and Health as soon as I arrived home, which I was glad to do.

We spent several pleasant and profitable afternoons and evenings discussing Christian Science, and by the time we were ready to start upon our return journey my traveling companion's enthusiasm and natural kindness of heart would not allow him to pass by the least chance of proving the healing power of Truth, and many minor ills were met and mastered.

Upon our return journey, I met a young man on the train who had been to Phœnix, Arizona, seeking health through the climatic belief. He was now on his way home, discouraged and hopeless. I had not much time to tell him of the living Christ before our paths took opposite directions, he going north through California, while my route was through New Mexico and Colorado. I have never heard from him, but did the best I could to give him hope, and point the way.

Our train was delayed for fourteen hours at Albuquerque, New Mexico, because of a bridge having given way, and while we were waiting, my friend decided to take a look through the train. A short time after, he returned and told me that he had met a lady in the car ahead who was interested in Christian Science, and that she was trying to cheer up a traveler who was sick almost unto death, and was fearful that she would not be able to bear up until she arrived home, because of the long delay. I promised my friend that I would investigate matters and see what could be done, and a few moments later I entered the forward car, and my attention was attracted to two ladies seated together; one of them was bolstered up into a sitting position with pillows, and the other was talking very earnestly to the sick one. As I passed I heard the one lady say, "I wish I had a copy of Science and Health with me." I did not stop, but walked to the end of the car, then turned back, and went to my seat and secured my Science and Health and, returning to the lady, I said, "I heard you express the desire for a Science and Health; here is one." She took the book and with much feeling thanked me and asked me if I would sit with them for awhile. Then she asked me if I was a practitioner, and I told her that I was. She could not hold back the tears of gratitude, as she said, "Oh, how I have desired that some one with more understanding than I would come and give this dear sister hope!"

The invalid was on a return trip from a sojourn in the mountains somewhere in the southern part of Arizona, where her home physician had advised her to go to seek health, but there had been no gain, and now her only hope and desire was to live long enough to reach her home near Kansas City, and pass out of this life with her husband and children by her side. She had attempted the return trip feeling that if all went well her strength would last long enough to carry her through, and now this long fourteen-hour wait had so discouraged her that she felt sure that she would not be able to retain consciousness until she arrived at her destination. The lady who was seated with her explained that she had noticed that the woman was failing fast, and had introduced herself, and was doing what she could to bring hope back to the heart that was hopeless.

That fourteen-hour wait was the shortest fourteen hours of the entire four days' trip to those that were interested in the sick lady. In fact, I lost all reckoning of time in my earnest desire to help her. I talked and treated alternately all the afternoon and late into the night. She gained perceptibly under my efforts, and in the morning I was up early and again began treatment. About half-past seven my friend and myself went into the car ahead to see how the patient had fared during the night; she was still in her berth, but the other lady was up, and I left word with her not to disturb our friend, but to let her sleep as long as she wished.

About half an hour later we went again into the forward car, but she had not yet risen, and the porter was becoming much alarmed, thinking that perhaps she had passed on during the night. I did all I could to assure him that she was all right, and that I was taking care of her. He then asked me if I were a doctor. I smiled and said that some of my friends call me one. This seemed to satisfy him for the time being, but a half-hour later he insisted that we call to the patient, to make sure that she was yet in the land of the living. I was not in the least uneasy, as I had noticed a steady gain all the afternoon and evening before, and I was sure that she was sleeping peacefully, and that she would feel much better when she awoke; but to quiet the fears of the porter I told her lady friend to part the curtains of the berth and call her. There was a hearty response at once, and the porter heaved an audible sigh of relief.

After she had had breakfast I again talked with her and she told me that she had not wakened during the night and that she had not had an entire night's sleep like the one just past for months and months. Hope was now high and there was no more thought of death before her arrival home, but thinking the relief only temporary, she hardly dared to think that she might ultimately be entirely healed. In our conversation she said, "You know, Mr. Walter, tuberculosis in its last stages, as my case is, can not be cured." I did all I could to disabuse her mind of this falsity and kept on with the treatment, and the following day when we arrived in Kansas City she was able to take care of herself and walked unaided out of the car and through the long train-shed into the depot. The parting at the depot affected us all keenly. I promised to continue treatment for the balance of the day, and having given her the names of the practitioners of her home town, obtained from the Christian Science Journal, a copy of which I had with me, she promised to take treatment from a practitioner in her home town at once.

Later I received a letter from her stating that she was making great progress and thanking me again for the help I had given her.

CHAPTER VI.

Upon my arrival home my dear wife rejoiced exceedingly with me, when I told her of the many demonstrations of the power of Truth over error, and again our hearts went out to our beloved Leader for having given us the means whereby we had become acquainted with the living Christ, the Truth that sets men free. I had gained much in the work that I had accomplished on this trip, and felt fully repaid for the time and effort spent in reflecting the healing Truth to those in need.

It was shortly after my return, that a dear friend, a Christian Scientist from a neighboring city, visited me, and one day as I was showing her about the yard, she noticed a cherry tree that was nearly stripped of its leaves, and asked me the reason for this destruction. I informed her that the tree had become infested with a small worm which had spread itself over the entire tree, and that I feared it would be ruined. I then and there received a friendly rebuke that taught me a much needed lesson. These were her words: "You are not much of a Christian Scientist if you allow a little thing like a worm to destroy your cherry trees. You have the power of the Word, why don't you get to work and save that poor tree from its enemy?" For a moment the thought came to me to say that I did not know that Christian Science would help in such a case, but I at once recognized that this was not true. I had merely not thought to apply it in this case.

She then told me of a beautiful vine that had been for several years growing in her yard until it had covered much of her porch, and that the previous year her attention had been called to the fact that its leaves seemed to be drying up and the vine dying, as was also a similar vine of her neighbors. She then told me that she had treated the vine and that soon she saw that a new lot of leaves were growing out to take the place of those that had fallen off, but the neighbor's vine, which had not been treated in Christian Science, had not recovered. I determined to try this method for the restoration of my cherry trees and the same evening started the work. A few days later all the remaining leaves of the tree and all the worms fell to the ground, but I kept on with my work and soon there was an entire new crop of foliage, and to-day that tree is as thrifty as any of its neighbors. I had learned the lesson that all things were amenable to the Christ Truth.

About this time I also learned another lesson. I was passing the door of a neighbor, a young married couple, the lady being somewhat interested in Science, but the husband was not, although he was not opposed to his wife's reading the literature. A few days previous to the day of which I am speaking a child had been born to them, and the little one seemed to have trouble in urinating. In fact, although this was the fourth day it had not yet urinated and the parents were becoming alarmed. I was requested by the anxious mother to come in and see the babe. I did so, and found there were present besides the parents the two grandmothers of the child. The young mother asked me if I thought I could do anything to relieve the condition, and I told her that Truth was all-powerful, and asked all those present if they had any objections to my treating the babe through Christian Science. There being none, I treated the child and also treated the mother for fear; I then waited half an hour, but there was no response to the treatment. I then treated again, this time taking into account the thought and fears of the wife's mother, and again waited a half hour, but still there was no response. Then through questioning I found that the father of the child had been similarly afflicted at birth, and that his mother had the thought that such things were of a hereditary nature. I again gave treatment, this time taking into account the thought of the husband's mother, and before I had fully finished my treatment there was a full and complete response.

Through the application of Truth I had broken the mortal law of heredity, which was holding this case, and when this had been accomplished the divine law which is ever present, was again in evidence, and perfect action was manifest. The lesson that I learned from this was the necessity of taking into account the erroneous thought of those surrounding any patient. I had been aware of this before, but not until this case was it forcibly proven to me.

The power of right mental activity on animals, our four-footed friends, was forcibly demonstrated to me in a case that I will now relate. My niece is the proud possessor of a beautiful Maltese cat, and for some time it had been noticed that pussy was not as playful or lively as usual and that she was shedding her hair. A careful examination was then made and it was discovered that she had a number of sores on her head and body and that her eyes were also very much inflamed. The evening following the discovery of the cat's illness my niece and her mother paid me a visit, and as they were also students of the healing Truth, they asked me how best to handle the disease. I explained to them in a general way, but they did not seem to grasp the import of what I said, and suggested that I give the cat an oral treatment. To show them the trend of right prayer I consented, and gave the requested oral treatment to the full extent of my understanding, and with a clear perception of the Truth. The remainder of the evening was spent in talking of the wonderful power of Truth, and it was quite late when they went home, and because of the lateness of the hour they did not give pussy any treatment. In the morning when feeding the cat it was noticed that she was much livelier than usual and upon examination they found that she was healed. The positive oral treatment of the evening before having been manifested in the cat's restoration to perfect health.

Another incident that showed me the wondrous power of right or correct thought was forcibly brought to my consciousness one afternoon as I was sitting on my porch. As I sat there in undisturbed peace doing my work, I heard shrieks of delight and childish laughter, and I glanced in the direction from whence the sounds came. I saw a man perhaps forty years of age, half-way down the block, lying at full length on the sidewalk. It was apparent to me from his peculiar actions in attempting to rise that he was very much intoxicated, and had no doubt lost his equilibrium and fallen prone upon the sidewalk, much to the amusement of the half dozen youngsters that had been watching his antics from a safe distance across the street. After repeated attempts to rise, and just as I was about to go to his assistance, the man, by the aid of a small tree that stood near by, regained an upright position. He stood still for several moments, trying to get his bearings, then again attempted to walk, but was unable even to stand, and just as he was about to fall again, by a special effort he managed to lunge upon a doorstep, and thereby saved himself from falling at full length.

He slowly straightened himself up into a sitting posture and buried his face in his hands. I watched him sitting there quietly for several minutes, and as he made no further attempt to walk I also seated myself, and my thought naturally turned to the unraveling of this man's error. I was not conscious of treating him, but was thinking of the absurdity of the claim that any liquor could dispossess man of the gift of God, the power of clear thought. Calmly and carefully I mentally sifted the wheat from the chaff regarding his seeming condition, with no special intention of helping him. A few minutes later, when I had finished thinking on the subject, I inadvertently glanced in his direction, and as I did so I saw him slowly but steadily rise to his feet, and with a motion much as though he was shaking himself, he straightened himself up and a moment later began to brush the dirt from his clothes. When he had finished he started to walk up the street past my home, and as he neared the place where I was sitting I took particular pains to see if he staggered, but I could detect nothing of the kind. He continued his walk up the street with no visible signs of his previous drunkenness. I did not know the man, neither did I speak with him, as I considered it unnecesary, for his actions proclaimed in unmistakable signs that he was free from his previous belief of drunkenness.

Whether the man or myself or the group of children that had stood laughingly by, was the most surprised I can not say; I certainly was surprised, but not until I had sat in silent contemplation for more than half an hour was I fully aware of what had healed the man, and when the full realization came I was all but overcome with adoration, wonder and awe at the power and impersonal nature of Truth, and at once I saw with a clearness never before attained the unbridgeable and unchangeable chasm between the Christ way, the healing and saving method of Jesus, and the methods of mortal mind, named by this mind hypnotism, suggestion, auto-suggestion, suggestive therapeutics, mortal thought transference, telepathy, and mental science, so-called; all these are temporal, of the earth earthy, mortal misconceptions, operated through and by the human will, in contradistinction to the everlasting emanations of divine Mind,

God, and the reflection of these emanations by individual consciousness.

My Leader, Mrs. Eddy, for my guidance, had written it plainly, in Science and Health, and this is where I first perceived it, though faintly, because of my blindness of heart; next my teacher had shown it to me, and I saw more plainly, yet, as it were through a glass, discolored with mortality. Now the ever-present Christ, Truth, because of the preparation of heart that I had previously experienced, showed himself as he really is, and I was able to perceive, at least in a degree, the living, active, ever operative Christ.

I was now aware that my Leader, Mrs. Eddy, had planted a seed of thought in my consciousness, which seed was impregnated with Truth, and as the eternal mandate of Mind is that each seed shall bear fruit after its kind, this seedling of thought sown by my Leader, would necessarily need to bring forth the fruit of Truth, providing I did not pervert or destroy that which she had sown.

Next my teacher had with painstaking care torn up and destroyed the weeds, which up to this time had been growing side by side with the seed of Truth, and now in this last impersonal demonstration at least one of the buds of promise had blossomed out into full flower, and its name is "wonderful." I know there are many more buds on this same bush, and I am doing all I can to live the life which will be conducive to an early blossoming of these buds of promise.

Slowly, though surely, the sense of poverty was being overcome more and more, and I was now looking to Mind as the source of all good, and that wonderful statement of the Master, "Seek ye first the kingdom of God, * * * and all these things shall be added unto you," was proving itself literally true in everyday life. I formerly often had said that I was born to be disappointed in the things I undertook, but I now could freely say, The Lord is prospering all things that I desire to accomplish. The old financial debts that had been for years growing greater had now been entirely liquidated, and I had money at hand with which to help my less fortunate brothers and sisters. I was not immensely wealthy in dollars and cents, but I knew that the source of all blessedness was able and would furnish me with all that I might rightly need or desire, and this knowing was the source of my riches and the extinguisher of my sense of poverty.

I began to improve my old home, making it more comfortable and more in keeping with my new vocation. A furnace, electric lights, bath, etc., were added and paid for when completed. I merely mention this to show that the words of the Master were literally true, as well as true metaphysically.

The second year of my experience in Christian Science was now drawing to a close, and my first book, "The Pastor's Son," would be ready for the printer's hands as soon as I could find someone whom I thought capable of looking it over carefully to eliminate any possible mistakes in statement as well as to seek out any errors of grammar that I might have overlooked.

Being new in this work, I was somewhat at a loss to know how to proceed, but at length a man was recommended to me who, I was told, was fully capable of doing the work I desired. The manuscript was given into his hands, and in a short time it was returned to me with a bill for his services. The work he did actually destroyed all that was good in the book, for he knew next to nothing of actual Christian Science, and the meaning that I wished to convey to my prospective readers was destroyed. This necessitated the re-writing of the whole manuscript, and when it was re-written I took it to the printers that had been recommended to me, and asked their advice regarding some one to look it over with the view of correcting the grammatical errors. I employed the one they recommended to me, and I did not give the book into the hands of any Christian Scientist at that time for correction in statement, my first experience in having it corrected being still too fresh in my mind.

I worked long and faithfully with the copy, striving to make it scientifically correct, but literary work was new to me, and so some minor errors were overlooked. The book had not been long on the market when divine Love met my need of a friend who could and would correct the simple errors that were in the first editions. The book was eventually revised by a master hand, and to-day is still in demand and fulfilling the mission that I sent it out to do—that is, it is telling the world of another book, that wonderful book of Mrs. Eddy's, "Science and Health, with Key to the Scriptures," through the study of which I am being liberated from the bondage of matter and the false law of mortality. That "The Pastor's Son" is surely fulfilling its mission is evidenced by many letters that I have received, of the same nature as the one that follows:

March 16, 1908.

Dear Mr. Walter—

I am glad that you are revising "The Pastor's Son." Not long ago one copy of "The Pastor's Son" was sent to a friend in a small town. As a result of reading this one book, six copies of

"Science and Health" have been sold. I know you are glad to hear all of these good things.

I am,

Your Co-Worker.

I have many hundreds of letters from individuals, telling of the help received, in the rolling away of the stone of materiality, through the book pointing so strongly to our text-book, Science and Health, from which I received my enlightenment.

In my practice I have had many cases that were similar in detail and such as are often given to the care of a practitioner; these I will not mention, but I will tell of a very unusual one that came to me early in my third year in Christian Science.

My home is about thirty-eight miles from the great city of Chicago, and one day my telephone rang, and as I placed the receiver to my ear I heard the operator say, "Chicago wants you." A few seconds later I recognized the voice of a very dear friend—one whom I had given treatment, and who had been much benefited thereby. She asked, "Is this Mr. Walter, of Aurora, the Christian Science practitioner?" I called the lady by name and told her I was ready to receive her message. She said, "It is not for myself that I called you up, but for a friend that lives in my house with me." She then gave me the lady's name, and told me that this friend had met with an accident. The evening before she had missed her footing and had fallen from a porch four steps high, and had broken a number of the bones in one foot. She said that her friend had at once telephoned to the practitioner who had on a previous occasion healed her of a serious illness, but found that she was not in the city, and the lady had been at a loss to know just what to do. Because of the insistence of her son, she had called in a physician, who, upon examination, said that the bones of the foot were broken, but that there was so much inflammation and swelling present that he could not then set the bones, and that he would need to wait until the swelling had subsided.

It was at this time that my friend suggested that she allow her to call me up over the phone; to this she consented, and I took the case. I later ascertained that the pain was eased in a very short time and the swelling began to subside. She had no trouble in falling asleep, and slept peacefully the entire night.

The next morning the pain was entirely gone and the swelling very much reduced by the time the doctor called.

The son insisted that he set the bones, but the mother and my friend were firm in their objections, and would not hear to his touching the foot.

A few days later she had the full use of the injured member, and asked permission to come to my home to see me, wishing to thank me in person for the good work that had been done; a few days later we met for the first time, and, according to her own statement, there was no visible sign, either to the sense of sight or to the sense of feeling, that she had ever had an accident. This occurred several years ago, and I have often been in correspondence with her during this time, and there has never been an indication that the healing was not perfect and permanent, according to her own statement.

Another case in which both the bone and muscle were supposed to be affected was presented to me for healing, and as this came to me in a way a little out of the ordinary, I will relate it here:—

I had promised my brother-in-law and three other friends an automobile trip of two or three days' duration, through the lake region along the boundary line between the states of Wisconsin and Illinois, and on our first day we reached ———, Illinois, in the early evening, and decided to stay there for the first night. I have a sister living there, and had written her that we would stop for a short time at her home, it being our intention to go to the hotel for accommodations, but upon our arrival we found this sister fully prepared to give us all a hearty welcome and a supper that was nothing short of a banquet, and both my sister and my brother-in-law would have it no other way but that we make our home with them during our stay. The house was large and there was plenty of room.

My sister's family consists of one daughter, now a young married woman, and one son, who was then twenty years of age. This young man, some time before, had in some way injured his arm and had been under the regular physician's care, and at the time of our visit his case had reached a critical state, but so well did he conceal his discomfort that I did not detect the great suffering and pain that he was enduring. I could see that he was very weak and much emaciated, and remarked about it, and was informed that it was because of the loss of sleep; but still I did not become conscious of his terrible need. His courage and fortitude were wonderful, but during the night I awoke and thought I heard some one walking and also a half-suppressed groan; I listened intently, trying to locate the sound, but there would be a long silence, followed again by a groan. I had decided that if I heard it again I would get up and investigate, but having been out in the wind all day, I was not as wakeful as usual, so fell asleep, and when next I awoke it was daylight.

Upon arising I made inquiry as to whether any one else had heard the groaning, but none of my friends had heard it. Later I asked my sister if any one had been sick during the night, and she informed me that her son had not slept for more than a few minutes at a time for more than two weeks, and that he frequently walked the floor for hours at a time, and nothing that they were able to do seemed to relieve him. I at once asked why they had not told me of this before, as I was aware that my sister was a believer in Christian Science healing, and also read much in Science and Health. I was then informed that the father, while not opposed to Christian

Science, thought that it would be of no avail in such a case as his, and that they had been for some months doctoring with their family physician, and lately, at his advice, had been to see a specialist at Milwaukee. He had been trying to give relief, but with no better success, and it had now arrived at the point where an immediate operation was advised, as the specialist was fearful that if the disease was not soon arrested that he would lose his arm.

I said nothing further to my sister on the subject, but when I was ready to leave I went to my nephew himself and calling him by name, said, "I will be back home in Aurora in two days, and you are perfectly welcome to come down and visit my son for a few weeks, and while you are there I will see that that arm is healed; you do not need an operation, neither do you need to suffer this pain. Will you promise to come?" His answer was a decided "Yes, I will come."

The morning after my arrival at home he came. He was so weak that he could scarcely stand;

his arm was in a sling and in a voice made weak from much suffering he slowly told me that he had not slept a moment since he had seen me last, which was more than fifty hours before. During luncheon his eating was a mere pretense, and the little that he did eat he found great difficulty in conveying to his mouth because of weakness and also because the arm that had not been injured was becoming affected, presumably through sympathy.

As soon as luncheon was over he asked to be shown to his room, as he wished to lie down and rest if possible. I began treatment at once, and later in the afternoon he again made his appearance and reported that he felt stronger and that the pain was not quite so severe, but that he had not been able to sleep.

About eight o'clock that evening he retired for the night, and in the morning reported that shortly after retiring he had fallen asleep and had slept for more than ten hours without awaking. We ate breakfast and a few hours later he again went to his room and slept until luncheon time, and also slept the greater part of the afternoon; this continued for the first three or four days, much to the disgust of my son, who had anticipated a good time in this visit of his cousin. My son said, "I don't see why he wants to sleep all day and all night, too; we haven't had a bit of fun." I assured him that this sleeping would not continue much longer, and the fifth day the young man was so much improved that he decided to take a walk about our city, and from that day the gain was even more rapid than before, and in a short time all soreness and weakness was gone from the arm and he again had the full use of that member.

Just what had caused the injury the young man could not tell me, but his thought was that it had come through playing baseball, and that in the first place it was supposed to have been a tearing away of the muscle of the arm from the bone; at any rate, the muscles that are always found on the upper side of the arm, where the arm joins the shoulder, had shifted their position until at the time I started treatment they hung limp and useless, in a position closer to the under side of the arm than to the upper side. I was further informed that while under the regular medical doctor's care the flesh from which the ligaments had been torn had become diseased and had commenced to make the bone carious, and it was for the purpose of scraping the bone to remove this disease that the operation had been suggested.

It is several years since this occurred, and only a few months ago I saw my nephew, and he assured me that the arm was absolutely healed, and that it was much stronger than ever before, the muscle being also in its normal place.

An X-ray photograph was taken of this arm by the specialist, in the endeavor to find out just what the matter was, and what was best to do, and it was after this photograph was taken that the specialist advised the operation. I merely mention this to forestall the threadbare statement I have often heard after Christian Science has been successfully used, which is this: "There wasn't anything serious the matter, or the case would not have been healed through Christian Science effort." But the fact remains that according to mortal thought and in accordance with it, there was enough in this case to warrant the attending physician to recommend an operation if the arm was to be saved.

It is also true that according to the Science of Being there was not anything the matter, the patient merely suffering from a belief, and it was this belief that was manifested in the arm, as a very badly diseased bone. The difference in the method of the removal is also clearly seen, in that the specialist recommended that the arm be cut open and the diseased matter (effects of belief) be scraped from the bone. He paid no attention to the belief in the patient's consciousness, which was the erroneous and procuring cause, while I paid not much, if any, attention to the externalized effect of the belief (the disease), but put all my time to the removal of the belief from the consciousness of the patient, knowing that which the specialist did not know—that if I were able to remove the belief (the erroneous cause) from the consciousness of the patient, the effect (the disease) must also disappear, as surely as a spot of sunlight which is being reflected on the wall from a small mirror will and must cease when the cause of the spot of reflected sunlight (the mirror) is taken away; for that which was seen on the patient's body and which *materia medica* called carious bone, etc., was but the visible reflection of the belief of such a condition in the thought of the patient, or of the physician, or of general mortal mind.

CHAPTER VII.

I have had many cases of so-called appendicitis presented to me for healing, but this very little error with the very big name has always yielded to my efforts so easily that I thought at first not to mention it at all; but when I think of the widespread belief in this disease, and its many fatal results, I have concluded to cite one case which is perhaps an average one. My telephone rang; I answered, and here is the message that I received: "Mr. Walter, my wife requested me to call you up and ask you if you think that you can help her; she is suffering from a severe case of appendicitis, and as this is the third attack, we are very fearful of the outcome, as the third attack is very often fatal." I asked the speaker's name and he gave it me, but I did not know him; I had met his wife, the patient, once or twice.

On further questioning I was made aware that

his wife was a nurse, and knew so much of the fatal results of a third attack and also the great danger attending an operation for appendicitis, that, although all preparations had been made to take her to the hospital that day, to be operated upon, she had hesitated and had at the eleventh hour, as it were, decided to try Christian Science treatment. I was further informed that the time set for the operation was at ten o'clock that day, and it was about seven o'clock the same morning when the call came. The husband knew nothing at all about Christian Science at that time, he never having given it a serious thought; hence he was not nor could he have been in favor of this method of treatment, but being a very good and conscientious man, he had called me merely because his wife had wished it.

I took the case, but instinctively felt that if there was no improvement by ten o'clock that the operation would be performed. I determined then and there that surgical means for her relief would be unnecessary, and immediately applied myself to the solution of the problem; there was response at once and by ten o'clock the improvement was so great that the patient no longer thought of an operation, and by noon of the same day she was well enough to have prepared the noon-day meal if it had been necessary; in fact practically all the symptoms of the disease had disappeared. This occurred three years ago, and there has been no return of the trouble.

This demonstration of the healing power of Truth awakened this nurse to such a degree that she at once paid me a visit and after a few private talks she entirely renounced the drug method of healing, and began a careful and systematic search for Truth, and later she was able to preach the Gospel and heal the sick in the Christ way, the way our Leader has set forth in the Christian Science text-book. She has to my own knowledge through the application of Truth healed many diseases that *materia medica* calls incurable, and she is devoting practically all her time to the healing work and the study of Christian Science.

She has also become a member of the local Christian Science Society and is a member of the Mother Church and a class student.

Another case of a nurse that came to me for healing, might be of interest. A practical nurse, and a graduate also, had been for a number of years attending the sick in the city of Chicago, and while upon a case of tuberculosis was attacked by this dread disease. She consulted her favorite physician, and later a specialist of this disease, but the only consolation they could offer after repeated efforts to heal her, was that she go to her home, which was in the country, and make the best of her remaining years, for she knew nearly as well as her physicians the usually fatal nature of the disease she had contracted, and especially since her case was one of the type known as quick consumption.

When I met her the glands on both sides of her neck were much enlarged, and all the other regular symptoms of the disease were present. I gave her seven weeks of Christian Science treatment and then she was, as far as she herself could discover, entirely healed; she discontinued treatment and went on a long trip to visit her father and mother.

Months later I met her again and she assured me that at some time in the future she hopes to devote her entire time to Christian Science and its healing work. According to the letters I have received, there has been no return of this disease or any of its symptoms.

During all this time my book, "The Pastor's Son," was called for more and more, and letters of gratitude for help received from it were present in almost every mail. Many were the requests that I write more, and many asked for a catalog of all my works. I answered this call by writing down my thoughts at odd times and eventually worked them into story form. This is how and why "The Doctor's Daughter" was written. It is a sequel to "The Pastor's Son", and from the demand for it I am led to believe it is fulfilling the mission for which it was written.

But it seems to me as I stop to review the last few years, that the more successful I became in my healing and writing, the busier Madam Gossip became, and like the nature of gossip, the accusations were ever changing. When in a few instances I tried to trace this to its head, the thread ended in my home town. Truly, "A prophet is not without honor save in his own country."

Not that I wish to intimate that I have no friends in my home town; far from it. The fact is that because Truth has destroyed so many cases of disease through me, I have so many friends, and they are staunch and true, too, that often I am at a loss to find time to help them all, and I can clearly see that the best way to permanently do so is to show them the way to help themselves, and make them stand upon their own footing at the earliest possible moment. Some resent this in a mild way at first, but soon they see the wisdom of this method and thank me for having insisted that they first try to work out their own problems before they bring them to me for solution.

The next case that I will speak of taught me the lesson that all Christian Scientists ought to be careful not to make statements, especially in public, that the one addressed cannot understand, for in so doing one often places a stumbling-block instead of a stepping-stone. The case I have in mind was that of a young lady who was not much interested in Science, although she had heard much of it, as she had a friend who was a staunch believer. This young lady had come to see my wife regarding some needle-work, of which art my wife is considered quite an expert, and upon the afternoon in question, shortly after her arrival, she complained of severe pains in the stomach, and informed my wife that she thought it best to return home at once, as she had not brought her medicine with her Mrs. Walter suggested that she allow her to call me, and that I would give her a Christian Science treatment, and then she would not need to go home for the medicine, but to my wife's surprise the young lady answered, "No Christian Science for me." When asked the reason, she said, "Your husband would merely tell me that my stomach does not ache, and I know that it does." When asked for a further explanation the lady said, "About three weeks ago I had a similar attack and it became so severe that I was obliged to ask my employer to allow me to go home, and as I entered the street-car I noticed a friend who was a beginner in Science sitting alone, and I seated myself beside her; as I did so she noticed that I was in pain and asked me what was the matter, and when I told her that I had severe pains in my stomach and was then on my way home, she said, 'Your stomach doesn't ache; it can't ache. Don't you know that matter has no sensation?' I was so disgusted with the woman that I arose and went to another seat, without making her any reply, and if your husband is a Christian Scientist, and I know he is, he will merely tell me something of this same nature, and I think I am capable of knowing for myself as to whether or not my stomach is paining me."

My wife merely smiled and said, "I am going to call Mr. Walter, and then we will see what he will say," and coming to my office door she called me and told me of the suffering of the lady. I went into the parlor where she was seated and asked her if she would object to my giving her a silent treatment. She said she had no objections, but that she had no faith in Christian Science. I merely answered, "I have, and I am going to prove my faith by my works," and at once commenced the silent treatment. I think I treated her for about fifteen minutes, then without a word left the room and went back to my work in my office. I was sure that my wife, whose understanding was growing wonderfully, would say all that it would be necessary to say to her.

About two hours later the lady rapped on my office door and when I opened it she said, "Mr.

Walter, I thank you for having given me that treatment, for the pain all left while you were yet treating me, and there has been no return of it since, and I wish to add that if that is Christian Science I want more of it." In her hand I saw that she had a copy of the Christian Science Sentinel and a copy of the Christian Science Journal, besides some other reading matter, and I knew from this that my wife had done all that was necessary to put her on the right road.

While the statements that the lady on the street-car made to this young lady were true (there being no sensation in matter, as I fully proved through my treatment of this case), yet the assertion was untimely, and instead of being helpful it merely awoke resentment on the part of the one she intended to benefit; and if things had not happened just as they did, she might have carried this prejudice for years, thus shutting out from herself the healing Truth, merely because of an untimely statement of a friend.

Our Leader tells us in "Science and Health,"

page 414, line 15: "To fix truth steadfastly in your patients' thoughts, explain Christian Science to them, but not too soon,—not until your patients are prepared for the explanation,—lest you array the sick against their own interests, by troubling and perplexing their thought." Also on page 396, beginning on line 22, we may read: "At the right time explain to the sick the power which their beliefs exercise over their bodies. Give them divine and wholesome understanding, with which to combat their erroneous sense, and so efface the images of sickness from mortal mind." Again, on page 417, line 27, our Leader states: "Explain audibly to your patients, as soon as they can bear it, the complete control which Mind holds over the body."

It will at once be apparent from the above quotations taken from our text-book that there is a right time to make statements of Truth to patients, and to those who are seeking the Christ Truth, and therefore it were wise if the beginner in Christian Science would not allow himself to be carried away by his zeal or enthusiasm to make assertions that are not easily understood by non-Scientists, as much misunderstanding can come from a partial or unwise statement given to those who are not yet ready for the meat of Christian Science.

The apostle Paul says in I Corinthians III, 2, "I have fed you with milk, and not with meat: for hitherto ye were not able to bear it, neither yet now are ye able", clearly showing that there is need for caution in explaining truth to the beginner. Still we must not be so overcautious that we hide our talent in the ground, or selfishly try to gain truth from others, and never give any in return, for the Infinite is seeking channels for expression, and to those who express most and correctly, most will be given.

I shall now relate a case which came to me at about the close of my third year in Christian Science and will first show how a little, kindly act may be rewarded by a large return of blessings.

One day while I was away from home there came a call for healing from a gentleman who had run the gauntlet of *materia medica* and who, according to mortal belief, was very ill. At the time in question I had so much healing work before me that I felt it impossible to take on any more cases until those who had already applied had been healed and so had fully decided not to take this gentleman's case, but when I acquainted my wife with my intention she said, "Surely, you will not turn away Mr. ——!" I remarked that I could see no special reason why I should take his case. She then called to my remembrance an incident which happened many years before and which I had entirely forgotten. The incident was this: One day this man in the kindness of his heart, when meeting my wife on the street, told her of a small sum of money which was coming to her and which she had supposed was lost, and acquainted her with the fact that if she would make application for it he would see that she would receive it. We followed the advice of this kind and honest gentleman and were rewarded by receiving the said sum; and now my wife was interceding in his behalf, stating that one good act deserves another. I therefore reconsidered my intention and called upon the gentleman, the outcome being that I took his case for treatment, even though I knew that this would necessitate my working late into the night, but would not have done so had he not done the little act of kindness years before. Another reason for my mentioning this case is that in the handling of it I learned more of the all-knowing nature of divine Mind.

I started treatment and the response was apparent at once, and at the expiration of five or six days the patient asked me whether it would interfere in any way with his recovery if he would take a trip which he had long contemplated to a summer resort at one of our inland lakes. I told him that I saw no reason why he could not be healed at a distance as well as at his own home, because the one Mind was everywhere present.

A day or two later he departed on his trip. He had told me the name of the lake and place where he was going and because of similarity of the name of the lake with that of a lake in another state there was an error in my thought regarding the place to which he went. My thought was that he had gone to a lake in Wisconsin, whereas the place to which he went was in the state of Indiana. I recollect distinctly that when I treated him I thought of him as being at a lake in Wisconsin, but the all-knowing or divine Mind was not so deceived, for under my treatment this man was restored to health at the lake in Indiana where he was staying.

This incident proved conclusively to me that whereas mortal sense might be mistaken or deceived, the divine Mind, being all-knowing, could not be deceived. This healing was also an added proof to me that it was the divine Mind that heals, and that suggestion was a fallacy, for had

I used the method of the suggestionist or the theory of the telepathist, I would have attempted to consciously direct or throw out thought suggestions to my patient as being at a lake in Wisconsin and thereby wasted my effort.

Thus far in this book I have dealt almost wholly with the physical healing that follows as a direct result of the application of Christian Science and to those who view it from the outside, the healing effect seems to mortal sense to be the greatest blessing to be derived from the application of Christian Science, but that this view is not entirely correct can readily be ascertained by speaking with those who are conscientiously endeavoring to live the life of a Christian Scientist. In reality the greater blessing is the spiritual uplift, the mental freedom from those old enemies named fear, worry, doubt, anxiety, envy, anger and hate, for although it is much to be free from bodily ills yet life in its best and noblest sense cannot be enjoyed while the mental realm is in possession of the above named army of arch-conspirators against man's peace and happiness. In my own case it meant much to me to be freed from the almost ceaseless pain which had been with me for years, but not until I had advanced to the point where I found that the kingdom of peace and harmony was within, did the greater blessings of Christian Science come into my life, and in a degree I saw the ultimate of Christian Science.

At length I realized that there was not, that there could not be continued peace and happiness for me until I cast out of my own mentality anger, hatred, impatience and kindred thoughts, but when I began to fill the places that were occupied in former times by these thoughts, with thoughts of charity, loving-kindness and good-will towards all, I became acquainted, in a degree, with "the peace that passeth all understanding." I found by a careful self-examination that it was not the so-called large happenings that irritated and distressed me, but rather the little things, most of them so small that in moments of calm thought they would not even have been noticed.

In the handling of many patients I found that nearly always it was the trifling things that caused the discontents of life; for instance, the misplacing of a collar button formerly caused me more anger and trouble than the loss of a piece of property, and I found a similar condition of things to be present in nearly all cases presented to me for healing. I have seen an employer grow white with passion because an employee had carelessly dropped a ten-cent lamp chimney and broken it, but who, at another time, seeing an entire crate of dishes valued at several hundred dollars dropped and the contents shattered, merely said, "Never mind, boys, it could not be helped." I have seen a man turn away from his best friend in anger because of a chance word spoken at an inopportune time and bear malice toward this old-time friend for years afterward; but this same man at another time, when another friend wrongly accused him of the vilest villainy, turned silently aside with only sorrow in his heart and in a short time he forgave the one who wronged him so cruelly but never forgave the honest, tried and true friend who had merely offended by a chance word. These are samples of the vagaries of the human mind, and it was the overcoming and casting out of such irritating influences as these that gave me the peace of mind that I had so longed for in the old life, but never was able to find.

Christian Science is also the greatest healer of grief and sorrow that has ever been placed before the world. In connection with this thought I will cite a case which came to my attention and which was quickly healed through the application of Christian Science. A young lady for some time betrothed to the choice of her heart happily awaited the time appointed for her wedding day, and was busily engaged in preparing the wedding trousseau when like a bolt out of a clear sky her intended husband was taken with an illness which quickly developed into mental aberration, necessitating his removal to his home town and later to commitment to an insane asylum. This young lady was heart-broken, and because of this seeming trouble her own happy smiles were soon a thing of the past and she began rapidly to fail in health.

It was at this stage that Christian Science was suggested to her by a friend and subsequently this led to her coming to me for treatment. She responded to treatment very readily and soon the broken heart was healed and health was restored and she became an ardent follower and loyal student of the Christ Science. When she first came to me she thought that her entire life was ruined, but since coming into Science she has found a more abundant sense of Life and happiness. Under ordinary circumstances the chances would have been much in favor of her leading a lonesome and sad life to the end of her days. In speaking with her later she told me personally that she considered the spiritual uplift to have been a greater blessing than the healing of her bodily ills.

To show that drunkenness is also overcome by a correct application of the Christ Truth, I will cite the case of a man who had for years drunk intoxicating liquor to excess, who after each debauch would be so ill-tempered that he made his home at such times a hell on earth for himself and also for the other members of the family. Christian Science was suggested to him as a possible cure for his degrading habit and soon he was a diligent student of our text-book. There was constant gain from the very first in his case, and although there were frequent backslidings yet the intervals grew farther and farther apart until the happy day arrived when all desire for strong drink had been met and destroyed. His entire life was changed and whereas in former times he would not have been considered a Christian even in the old thought, he is now an honest and earnest seeker for Truth and is now leading the life of a Christian and a true gentleman. I know of no means that could have wrought so great a change in a man's life as was wrought in this man's life, other than the application of the healing Christ. The spiritual uplift in this case was tremendous, the man having been lifted from a very low sense of existence to the life of a conscientious follower of the Christ.

CHAPTER VIII.

During the fourth year many calls for healing came to me; as a rule they were much like the general run of illnesses and diseases, but one of them more than the others stands out as proving the all-potency of a correct application of the Truth, for the healing of both mind and body.

The patient was a lady who had endured all the tortures of an emaciated and pain-racked body for fourteen long years, with hardly one day of cessation from pain, and she had also suffered much mental agony. In this case the suffering was so intense that the patient had not had a complete night's sleep for several years, and her limbs and arms were so inflamed that to move them without pain was impossible.

Treatment was commenced and continued for several months. This case yielded more slowly than any I ever treated, but in due time the physical healing took place and she arose from her bed of suffering and was able to slowly move about her home and to be wheeled about in a wheel-chair; a little later the wheel-chair was abandoned and at present she walks to all parts of our city and is well and strong and this dear woman, whose life had become embittered by the trials and ills of this earth's turmoil, has again been restored through the Christ, Truth.

Many write me, why am I not healed? I refer them to the Christian Science text-book, and especially to this paragraph: "Self-love is more opaque than a solid body. In patient obedience to a patient God, let us labor to dissolve with the universal solvent of Love the adamant of error,—self-will, self-justification, and self-love,—which wars against spirituality and is the law of sin and death." ("Science and Health," page 242, lines 15 to 20.)

Frequently I receive letters in which there is mention made of some specific ailment, and the question is asked, "Can you heal the ailment that

I have written about?" and the thought of time is forcibly expressed in that I am told to remember that this ailment has been of ten or twenty years' standing. These dear people think that it is a person that does the healing, but I always write them: "I can of mine own self do nothing:" St. John, 6:29; "My Father worketh hitherto and I work," St. John, 5:17.

The next case I will speak of is known to *materia medica* as gastric colic, and although this trouble is not considered fatal, yet if allowed to continue for any length of time it often terminates with fatal results, the danger point frequently being reached in so short a time as three hours.

The patient, a man, strong and of usual robust health, was on a certain morning at about nine o'clock, taken with a severe attack of this disease. He was in a store at the time transacting some business, but took the next street-car for his home, and by the time he arrived there he was in very severe pain, which was constantly increasing in violence. His wife, who, a short time before, had been healed in Christian Science and who had taken up the study of the Christ Truth, tried to allay the pain, but her understanding at this early date seemed insufficient for the overcoming of the trouble, so she decided with the consent of her husband to call on me, for I had helped her when she was ill. In answer to a hurried telephone call the lady was informed that I was out of the city, and would not return before evening. In this extremity not knowing what else to do she sent for one of the best physicians of our city, who made a careful diagnosis and pronounced the case a very severe one and the patient in grave danger. The wife asked the physician if he could not give the patient morphine to ease the pain, and his reply frightened her still more, for his answer was that the heart-action was so very bad that even a very small quantity of morphine might cause instant death. The physician further said, "I do not see that I can be of much help, but I will leave medicine." The patient took it after much persuasion, but could not retain it.

The wife now bethought herself of two Scientist friends, and asked their assistance, which was freely given, but there seemed to be no gain in the patient's condition; still I am of the opinion that if it had not been for the help of these two friends this man would have passed on before I arrived home.

As soon as I opened the door of my house, my wife told me of the case and I immediately called up this lady and in a few words she told me of the great trouble her husband was in. I requested her to tell the two friends that were then on the case that I would relieve them and begin treatment at once. In about twenty minutes I called the lady, feeling sure that the healing Christ was at work in the consciousness of the patient and I was not disappointed in her reply, for the paroxysms of pain were already less frequent and in a few more hours they were so far apart that he was able to catch a little sleep between them, and when morning dawned the danger was over. It required several days of treatment, however, before he was again as well and strong as usual. The pain must have been something terrible, for this strong man lost more strength and flesh according to mortal reckoning during this one day and night of pain than some that are sick for weeks. I am happy to be able to state that this good man and his wife are now members of the Mother Church and also of the local Christian Science Society and are loyal students of our text-book; the wife having taken class instructions, is busily employed in the field of healing and saving, and with very good results.

The fifth year of my Christian Science experience was one of constant unfolding of the Truth that makes free, and is similar to the other years of which I have told, but the healings in general were accomplished more quickly, which is accountable in that I am striving more and more to live a better and better life, and also because my constant study of our text-book and the practical application of what it teaches has given me a better understanding of the changeless Principle that we call God.

Feeling that I have already mentioned enough and varied cases so that all who read this book will see that the Christ Truth, as explained and exemplified in the Christian Science text-book, is applicable to the healing of all manner of disease, regardless of name, symptom or the length of time that the disease has been in evidence, I will cite but a few of the many healings following my efforts of the fifth year.

I will first make mention of the case of a lady suffering with a large and painful abscess. When she came to me she had been unable to sleep for several nights preceding, because of the intense pain. Treatment was given and the response was immediate, the patient resting well the first night and at the end of a few days the abscess was a thing of the past. This lady is a very good and conscientious student of our text-book, and her constant endeavor is to have and to know the Mind of Christ.

As I have not mentioned a case of Bright's Disease and because this is classed with the incurable diseases, I will now briefly do so.

A man about thirty-five years of age came to my house and told me that his physician said that his ailment was Bright's Disease and that it was merely a matter of time as to when it would prove fatal, and having heard of some of my healing work from a relative he came to ask me what chances he had of being healed through Christian Science treatment. I assured him that no case was incurable to God and that in Christian Science, God was the only healer. That very day he bought a "Science and Health" and took it to his home in the country. At the end of a week he wrote me that there was considerable improvement, and at the end of the second week he wrote me that I could discontinue treatment, as he was entirely healed, which proved to be the case, as I have seen him several times since and he is strong and healthy and there is not one symptom of the dread disease.

The next and last case that I will relate gives me more than ordinary pleasure because of the glorious results. It is as follows:

A lady sixty-eight years of age wrote me for treatment, the claim being one of long standing, perhaps twenty-five years; dyspepsia, indigestion, and general stomach trouble were the names given. I gave about ten days' treatment, and she was able to eat anything that she wished without the least inconvenience. Strength returned and she became as spry and active as many ladies of thirty.

A short time later this lady's husband, a man of seventy-six, came to me for treatment. His trouble was rheumatism, with which he had been a constant sufferer for years, during which time a strong cane was his constant companion. At the time of which I speak he was confined to his bed with a severe attack of this complaint and he could neither dress nor move about without assistance. The family doctor was called and after a diagnosis the case was found to be a complication of rheumatism and dropsy, and the thought went out that his time had about come. I was called and the case was given into my hands. The taking of medicine was stopped and Christian Science treatment begun. He responded quickly and in a few days was again able to dress himself and be about the house; at the end of a week very little could be seen of the former swelling and bloating of the hands and feet. At the end of two weeks' treatment he was practically healed and shortly after the much worn cane was discarded and there has been no need of it since, and he seems to be growing younger every day. This aged couple are constant readers of our German periodical, "Der Herold Der Christian Science," and also all our other German literature.

This all occurred about six months previous to the time set for the celebration of the golden wedding of this aged couple, and when the day arrived my wife and I and our son were the only ones outside of the family that were bidden to the wedding.

One of the gifts was a gold-headed cane, presented to the old gentleman, who did not wish to accept it, stating that he had no more use for a cane. He was not at ease until he was told that this one was merely for style and not for use.

After the wedding feast, when all had assembled in the spacious parlor, this aged couple walked arm in arm to the center of the room, and with much feeling the old gentleman said: "Children, I want you always to remember that if it were not for Christian Science there would not have been any golden wedding in this home." Tears of gratitude sprang to the eyes of the aged bride and groom, and also to the eyes of many others who heard this simple but eloquent testimony.

CHAPTER IX

In the foregoing pages I have related my experiences in the healing of practically all manner of disease, without the aid of any material means. There are thousands of others who are doing likewise. Is not this proof conclusive that the healing Christ, the healing Truth, is again known to be dwelling with men? The Christ-truth made practical is Christian Science; and, through the discoveries and labors of Mary Baker Eddy, for the first time in human history the Christ-truth has been reduced to a systematic statement and a teachable science.

Truth is revealed; then what need to fear? Remember the words of Jesus: "Ye shall know the truth, and the truth shall make you free." Christian Science teaches and proves by demonstration that heaven (harmony) is not a place, but a state of being; that it is a mental and not a bodily condition, a state of Mind and not of matter.

It has been fully proven to me, through study and practice, that there are not two primal causes called good and evil—God and devil—but only the one Cause, good. Neither could evil spring from good because of their opposite nature. Then evil must be a belief or supposition, for we know God, good, to be real. I have also further learned that, in reality, there are not two mental conditions, one harmonious, the other discordant, but that only the one condition, harmony, heaven, is the real, and that any seeming discordant condition is belief, supposition, an illusion of the senses. So, also, I learned, through the study of Science and Health, that there are not in reality two conditions of health,—the one, good health, the other, ill health; but that only good health is real, and that seeming ill health is belief and an illusion of the senses, and I have proven this to be true in the healing of several hundred cases of so-called diseases.

This proved to me that there are not two qualities or quantities in the universe, the one called Spirit, the other, matter; but only the one, Spirit. Real things are not made of matter; they are true thoughts, divine ideas. Matter is false belief objectified.

There are not in reality both poverty and plenty, but only the one, plenty. Poverty is an illusion or supposition, a suppositious condition of false sense, but not known to true consciousness.

"Seek ye first the kingdom of God and His righteousness, and all these things shall be added unto you." Seek ye the truth of Being, and your false sense of Life will fade into its native nothingness, leaving you in full possession of all things good.

There are not both love and hate, but only Love. Can all this be rationally proven? Yes, to all those who believe in a First Cause or God, from whom all that really is has originated. This subject is vast, and a careful study of the Christian Science text-book, Science and Health, with the other works of our Leader, Mrs. Eddy, is needed for a full and definite explanation of this subject. The Bible as a whole teaches, and Christian Scientists know by actual demonstration, that God, or the First Cause, is good, and not both good and evil. It ought to be self-evident that only good could come or proceed from a good Cause; then evil is not and cannot be real. If there are those who think that evil is real, because they seem to see it all about them, then I will say to them that the only pretense to reality that evil has is mere appearance or belief, and not the reality of fact or truth. Real things and conditions, like truth, are facts, and are eternal. Evil has no fixed condition or eternal duration, but its temporality is evident to all.

The Bible further teaches that God is Spirit, and the necessary consequence, that from a Spirit-Cause there could come no matter; for matter, as we all know, is the opposite, or, correctly speaking, the suppositional opposite, of Spirit. Jesus said that the Father (the First Cause) is perfect: then in fact and in truth it would be impossible for imperfection to come from perfection; therefore imperfection, like evil, must be nothing more than supposition and not fact or truth. From a perfect Cause could not come discord, but harmony; not ill health, but perfect health: then ill health is mere belief, supposition; and when belief, supposition, a lie, is recognized as a lie, its seeming reality vanishes.

Spirit, Mind, God, being perfect, and being all, there cannot in reality be two minds or two conditions of Mind, one discordant, sickly and hateful, the other perfect, harmonious and loving. Therefore, one or the other of these conditions, qualities or states of consciousness must be erroneous, unreal, mere supposition. It ought not to take much thought to decide which is fact and which is the seeming, if God, Cause, is admitted to be perfect and good.

The Bible command, "Choose you this day whom ye will serve," means that you are at liberty to live in the true consciousness, the consciousness of Truth, and be at peace, instead of seeming to dwell in the supposititious consciousness, in which there is no truth, but only mortal belief, opinion and supposition. Mortals are those who are believing themselves to dwell in this untrue or suppositional consciousness; and the way out is to deny that there is any reality to this seeming or suppositional life, and to make positive declaration and recognition of the truth of Being, that the true and good and enduring are the only facts of existence and the only reality. This will elevate thought, consciousness, out of the present mortal supposition about life and being into the truth about God, Life, Being; and the "old man with his deeds" will have been "put off" and consciousness will have "put on the new man," will have been "clothed upon" by a perfect state of Mind. Then consciousness will manifest Truth, God, and will be God's man, and will no more be mortal, but immortal and perfect as the one Mind, the Father, that governs all, is perfect.

SOME RESULTS OF MY LITERARY WORK.

As stated in the Preface to my first book, "The Pastor's Son," the motive for writing that story was to call attention to *another book,* "Science and Health," hoping in this way to acquaint a larger number with the Christ, Truth, as explained and taught in the Christian Science text-book.

The following are extracts taken from a few of the many hundreds of similar letters received by me and on file in my office. They show conclusively that my purpose, as above indicated, has been fulfilled, and that my work in this line has met with abundant fruitage, and a record of my first five years of experience in Christian Science would scarcely be complete without an insertion of some of these letters. The results which they evidence constitute part of the rich reward of earnest effort.

On page 234 of Science and Health, Mrs.

Eddy says: "Whatever inspires with wisdom, Truth or Love—be it song, sermon or Science—blesses the human family with crumbs of comfort from Christ's table, feeding the hungry and giving living waters to the thirsty."

I am willing that my books shall be measured by this test in the light of the letters which follow.

January 8th, 1909.

Dear brother in Truth,

Kindly send me one dozen each of "The Pastor's Son" and "The Doctor's Daughter."

Unhesitatingly, I can say that these two works stand alone in Science fiction in the strength of their pointing to our text-book. Many others have a love story or other material thread running through them, which seems the central point. Yours is "Science and Health," "Science and Health," while an unflagging interest is kept up.

Truthfully,

June 30th, 1908.

Dear brother in Truth,

In many respects the book is superior to any other work of fiction along Christian Science lines. I said to one lady, "If 'The Pastor's Son' had been read by me in 1896, a copy of 'Science and Health with Key to the Scriptures' would not have lain in my house unread from Christmas, 1896, to September, 1906, almost ten years."

Respectfully yours,

July 20th, 1909.

Mr. W. W. Walter,

Through the kindness of a friend, I have had the pleasure of reading your book, "The Pastor's Son." I wish it could be in every home. It would reach many that through prejudice will not read "Science and Health."

Respectfully yours,

November 24, 1908.

My dear friend,

"The Pastor's Son" is still in constant circulation, enlarging the understanding of its readers and bringing many to the study of "Science and Health" and the Bible, and always calling forth gratitude for the author.

Yours very sincerely,

April 29th, 1909.

Kind friend,

"The Pastor's Son" is one of the greatest missionary workers that I know of, and we know of quite a number of text-books which it has been the means of selling, where the people would not read the text-book before. About a week ago a lady called on mother. This lady, though not a Christian Scientist, always goes to the lectures, since mother persuaded her to attend one about two or three years ago. At about that time, she thought she would like to read "Science and Health," so mother let her have one, and after two or three weeks mother thought she would call and see what progress she had made. To mother's surprise, she hadn't opened it, and told mother so, saying she hadn't found time, so mother brought her book home. About a week ago, when this lady called, mother was talking to her about "The Pastor's Son," but she wouldn't buy it, and, as mother keeps one of her own, she loaned it to her. The next day the lady called up over the phone, asking, "Where do you get this book, 'Science and Health'? I want one as soon as I can get one. It certainly must be a wonderful book if it is still better than 'The Pastor's Son.' I never read a book that did me so much good as it has." Needless to say, she came right over and went to the Reading Room, purchased a five-dollar edition of "Science and Health," and is reading and studying every spare moment, and thinks it is a wonderful book. We have heard of so many cases similar to the above.

I am, your sister in Truth,

July 13th, 1908.

Dear friend,

I borrowed your book, "The Pastor's Son," and

I have been so benefited by reading it that I asked a sister, who was a little interested in Christian Science, to let me read it to her, for I knew it was just what she needed. She consented and was convinced of the truth of Christian Science, which I had been for ten years trying to get her to accept. She wishes me to send for the book for her, so that she can take it home with her and have it to refer to, as she says it makes the truth so clear to her.

Wishing you all success in your new work,

I am, Yours in Truth,

December 21st, 1908.

My dear brother in Truth,

I finished reading "The Doctor's Daughter" last evening, and I must say, it is simply sublime, and the principle of Christian Science is set forth clearly and logically. I thought of Rev. 19:1-6; for this voice bears witness to truth, viz., Christian Science. God seems to be using your books as a wedge to open stony hearts, for all that read them immediately turn to Christian Science and buy the book, "Science and Health, with Key to the Scriptures."

I am so glad of the way in which you handled the thought of "false science," the religion that is "just as good," the "climbing-up-some-other-way" thought, and above all the "mixing of the medical thought with Science" idea. I find a great tendency to do that here. I know it will open blind eyes to this pernicious practice. The books are genuinely good, both of them.

Yours in Truth,

December 8th, 1908.

Dear Sir,

I have thought of writing you for a long time, to thank you for the comfort and stimulation of thought which I have gotten from "The Pastor's Son." I have been using it as an aid to interest beginners in Christian Science. It is very effective.

I have found that, when I gave a friend a copy of your book and followed it up immediately with a copy of "Jewel," there has been created an immediate demand for "Science and Health."

I have struggled alone in this community for three years, wishing that some Scientist would come and help me interest my friends. I now consider my prayer answered by the arrival of the two books, "The Pastor's Son" and "Jewel."

With best wishes for you in your good work, I remain, Yours in the faith,

January 14th, 1908.

Dear Sir,

I send for a copy of your book, "The Pastor's Son." I think it is the most helpful story-book I own. I have studied Christian Science for three years and have been an earnest student of Truth; your book has been of great benefit to me and I wish to thank you for it.

Yours very truly,

January 11th, 1909.

Kind friend,

"The Doctor's Daughter" has arrived. I have read it and liked it very much indeed. It is certainly fine. It seems to me that it would cause all who read it to want to study all of Mrs. Eddy's books. The one sent to Mt. Sterling, Iowa, to a friend, brought the following word: "I received your present and read it just as soon as it came, and I think it fine. Many thanks." She has loaned it to her friends to read; so I feel that it is on its way to help awaken some one that is hungering and thirsting for the Truth, as explained to us in "Science and Health." Then we will rejoice. "Well done, good and faithful servant." I shall be pleased at any time to hear from "The Golden Thread."

"God will give it;
Christ will protect it;
Heaven will bless it."

Again I thank you.

In Life, Truth and Love,

August 26th, 1908.

Wm. W. Walter:

Dear brother in Truth,

I like this revised book very much indeed, and find that, as people read it, they like it much better than the first ones you put out. Your book, "The Pastor's Son," seems to be doing good. I know of a case here, a lady from Butte, Montana, who was led to read your book, and reading it gave her the desire to read "Science and Health," with the result that by the reading of "Science and Health" she was cured of a chronic disease. Her husband also has become interested. She has six brothers, and wants to make a present of "The Pastor's Son" to each. She buys one at a time, as she feels she can afford it. She came in yesterday for the second one.

Yours in Truth,

January 28th, 1908.

My dear Mr. Walter,

I have just finished reading your most excellent

book, "The Pastor's Son," which was loaned me by a friend to whom it was a gift, so I am unable to find where to purchase one, and the price. Will you kindly advise me as to the price per copy, and the nearest place where it can be obtained? I have been a Christian Scientist nearly two years, and have often wished for just such a book to give to those who seemed to be prejudiced against Christian Science, and I know this book is invaluable for that purpose.

Yours in Truth and Love,

August 20th, 1908.

Dear Sir,

I find that I do not have to urge people to read the book, for they find it so helpful that they want to go over it several times. My father and mother are aged eighty-two and seventy-two, respectively, and have come into Science within the last year, and they think "The Pastor's Son" the most helpful Science story they have read. My father had been a practicing physician for over forty years and has given it up, and sees its nothingness, and they are both seeking to know more of Truth and will come into the Christian Science Church. Wishing you continued success in the Cause, I am,

Sincerely yours,

January 13th, 1908.

Dear Sir,

If there is anything that will induce people to apply themselves more earnestly to the study and practice of the precepts laid down by our Leader in her text-book, I think your book, "The Pastor's Son," and the other new book, "Paul Anthony, Christian," certainly will, and I congratulate both writers. Yours truly,

October 1st, 1907.

Dear Sir,

Enclosed find money order for your book, "The Pastor's Son." I had the pleasure of reading it at Hutchinson, and want a copy of my own, for I feel that you have been very fortunate in thus answering questions that non-believers ask every day, and which it has been difficult for the beginner to answer.

Yours truly,

November 6th, 1908.

Mr. Wm. W. Walter:

Dear Sir,

Herewith find money order in payment for "The Pastor's Son," which you were kind enough to send me in advance of payment. I have been studying Christian Science for the past few months, and your little book has been read with great interest and benefit. I am sure it will lead many to the study of "Science and Health." I may say that I have found in Christian Science a great joy, comfort and peace. It surely is the "Pearl of Great Price." Yours truly,

May 17th, 1908.

Dear Sir,

I have been reading your book, "The Pastor's Son," and it has brought much light to me. I have been studying "Science and Health" for two years, and I am finding the Truth, and am truly grateful.

Yours truly,

October 13th, 1909.

Dear Sir,

I enclose money order, for which please send me a copy of "The Pastor's Son." I have been visiting in Macon, Georgia, recently, where I gave away the copy I had, after lending it to several people who were much pleased with it, and said they were going to order copies for themselves. There are a few Scientists here, and I am hoping to convert a number of people with your book, and I think it one of the clearest story-books on Christian Science I have read. If at any time you should write another book, let me know.

Yours truly,

January 3rd, 1908.

Dear Sir,

Please quote me price on "The Pastor's Son" in lots of six or more. I have read this book with great interest and want to place a few copies with friends, hoping thereby to get them interested in our text-book, upon which yours is based.

I am, very sincerely,

August 28th, 1909.

Dear Mr. Walter,

Both of your books, "The Pastor's Son" and "The Doctor's Daughter," are a great comfort to me. The fact that these stories embody the principle of our faith so clearly and attractively, particularly to the inquirer into Christian Science, makes them, to my thought, of great value. * * * Surely, it must be a great joy to you to know your demonstration has been one bearing such good fruit.

Your earnest co-worker,

September 7th, 1908.

Dear Sir,

It was with the deepest interest that I read your most helpful book, "The Pastor's Son," and as I am an invalid, earnestly striving to free myself from bondage, I feel that I gained a great deal of help and comfort from your splendid book, and I would like very much to possess a copy.

Yours truly,

October 27th, 1908.

Dear brother in Truth,

Your card is received, saying that your new book is out. Enclosed find check. I know that God will bless you in your work. "The Pastor's Son" has been so helpful to beginners in this blessed Truth. Your well-wisher,

July 13th, 1908.

Mr. Wm. Walter:

Dear friend,

I want to tell you that this book, "The Pastor's

Son," has been very helpful to me, and I know it has to many others. I loaned mine to one man who is just getting interested in Science, and he said that he considered it a very beneficial book, as it explains many things which he had never understood before and answers many questions that had come to him. I thought this so good that I must tell you of it.

Yours in Truth,

April 11th, 1909.

Dear friend,

For some time I have desired to drop you a line expressing my appreciation of "The Pastor's Son." In many instances that I know of, it has been a great help to turn thought toward right thinking, which we are learning, in Christian Science, is power. Others who are reading it find that it clears up many perplexing questions.

Sincerely,

December 11th, 1907.

Mr. Wm. W. Walter:

Dear brother in Truth,

The story is so well told that it will convince many not in the faith, of the beautiful truth which our dear Leader is teaching us.

Yours in the love and truth of Christ,

November 15th, 1908.

Dear brother,

Your book, "The Doctor's Daughter," is received, and I have read it and found it most interesting—equally as good as "The Pastor's Son." I feel that I have been benefited in reading it, and know that all who read it will find much light thrown on passages of Scripture heretofore not clearly understood by many. I am,

Yours in Truth,

June 26th, 1908.

Dear Sir,

I have just finished reading "The Pastor's Son,"

published by you. I want to read the book "Science and Health," by Mrs. Eddy. Will you inform me where I can buy it and what is the cost? I want to send for it. Trusting to receive an answer by return mail, I am,

Very truly yours,

January 10th, 1908.

Dear brother in the Truth that maketh free,

Please send me a half dozen of your book, "The Pastor's Son." It is doing a beautiful work for Christian Science, and I must express my gratitude for the light it embodies.

Yours in Truth,

August 15th, 1908.

Dear Sir,

Through Mr. —— leaving a copy of your book, "The Pastor's Son," with a friend of ours, we have had the pleasure of reading it, and consider it the best Science fiction yet published. It is so simple that it seems that the uninitiated in Science would derive much benefit upon reading it. Please forward us a copy.

Yours in Truth,

September 11th, 1909.

My dear Mr. Walter,

While in New York, I called on a practitioner, and he told me of your good book, "The Pastor's Son." I went to the bookstore, but was unable to get it, as they were all sold out, so I left my order to have one sent to me here. The book came yesterday. I finished reading it this morning, and I want you to know how much I admire it. I think it has made plain many things to me, and I am truly thankful for it. I wish everyone could possess a copy of "The Pastor's Son," and then much would be plain to them. I am not a member of the Church, but have been trying to understand Christian Science, and have been helped by it many times, but nothing has helped me like your book, and I just felt as though I wanted to write and thank you for publishing such a grand help.

Yours gratefully,

November 30th, 1907.

Dear Sir,

I am certain that all lovers of our text-book will be grateful to you for publishing this excellent work. Sincerely,

March 11th, 1908.

Dear friend,

One dear, good sister, who has been in Science for some years, told me Sunday last that, after reading "The Pastor's Son," she gained a better understanding of the spiritual import of the Scriptures. All that have read "The Pastor's Son" say that it has helped them in so many ways.

Yours in faith,

May 1st, 1910.

Dear Mr. Walter,

Your book, "The Pastor's Son," has so appealed to some Germans that I have thought perhaps it might be very helpful if translated into the German language. I am a German and a Christian Scientist, and would try to translate the book, if you give me the permission to do it.

Truly yours,

(Note.—I did not think it wise to have the book translated at present.—The Author.)

Mr. Wm. W. Walter:

Dear brother in Truth,

I received your book, "The Pastor's Son," and find it one of the finest of its kind. It seems to bring out the fundamental thought so plainly and concisely and is so convincing. I love the book so much that I feel that every Christian Scientist should own one to loan to friends.

Sincerely yours,

January 1st, 1908.

Mr. Wm. Walter:

Dear Sir,

Please tell me the price of those two volumes which you have published—"The Pastor's Son" and "The Doctor's Daughter." I have read the first volume, and think it grand. I think it is a good book to give people to read, as it starts them to thinking, and in time leads them to study "Science and Health," by Mrs. Eddy.

Yours truly,

February 13th, 1909.

Dear brother in Truth,

Many thanks for your kind letter, and the explanation of the story, which will make it all the more interesting, if that were possible. I rejoice that I had the first copy sent to this country. I read it to a dear little sufferer, who has been in bed for over sixteen years. It would have done you good to see the pleasure it gave her. I left it that she might have a second reading. Her sister sews to support them both. She read it while the sister sewed. You can picture the scene.

The Pastor's Son is a good young man, and many will follow in his footsteps and rejoice all the way, and walk carefully lest with careless feet they trample some rare jewel on their way. I call my book the little Pilgrim, because it has made so many journeys and never returned void. I hope soon to see another from your pen. You have proved yourself a good channel; so spin on, brother, still leaving the thread in God's hands.

We must all work to lead the dear ones to partake of this great feast that our beloved Leader has prepared for us, in giving us "Science and Health, with Key to the Scriptures," the best companion that the dear old Bible has ever had. It was so kind in you to send me the second copy. I will loan it to those who are too poor to buy one, and there are many such here. I am sure you will be pleased to have me do so. As we lighten the way for another to tread, a hand that is mighty repays us again. And the pure white dove of

Christian Science is welcomed by all, as it comes sailing along in the atmosphere of divine Love, with healing in its wings. Again thanking you for your kindness, and wishing you all success, I am,

Yours in the love and truth of our Lord,

THE END.

WORKS BY WILLIAM W. WALTER

The Pastor's Son—cloth bound. Price $1.60
The Doctor's Daughter—cloth bound. Price $1.60
The Arbiter of Your Fate—cloth bound $1.60
The Healing of Pierpont Whitney—cloth bound ... $1.60
The Unknown God—Vol. 2 Luke and John—cloth cloth bound. 400 pages. Price $2.00
The Unknown God—Vol. 1 Matthew and Mark—bound. 460 pages. Price $2.50
The Sweetest Story Ever Told—cloth bound $1.60
The Unfoldment—200 p., cloth bound. Price $1.75
The Sower, The Seed, The Soil—cloth bound $0.75
The Christ Way—Bristol cover $0.75
The Allness of Good—leather bound $1.50
Metaphysical Bible Lessons—paper cover $0.85
The Great Understander—Price $2.25

Plain Talk Series—

No. 1—Mental Practice
No. 2—Thinking
No. 3—Delusion
No. 4—Sculptors of Life
No. 5—Your Supply
No. 6—Harmony
No. 7—Fear
No. 8—Practitioner and Patient
No. 9—Business
No. 10—The Way
No. 11—Work
No. 12—Rest and Joy

Booklet 20 Cents Each

Common Sense Series—Price 15 Cents Each

No. 1—The Bible
No. 2—The Man Jesus
No. 3—The Kingdom
No. 4—The Hereafter
No. 5—The Pilgrim
No. 6—Human Belief
No. 7—Consciousness
No. 8—Reflection
No. 9—I Am
No. 10—The Word
No. 11—Mental Warfare
No. 12—Right Thinking
No. 13—Metaphysics
No. 14—The Natural
No. 15—Mistakes
No. 16—Ease
No. 17—Self Help
No. 18—The Healer
No. 19—Reason
No. 20—Understanding
No. 21—Parables
No. 22—Thy Faith
No. 23—Creeds and By-Laws
No. 24—The True Concept
No. 25—The Rejected Stone
No. 26—Born Again
No. 27—The Father
No. 28—The Son
No. 29—The Holy Ghost
No. 30—Utilize
No. 31—Perfection
No. 32—Purification
No. 33—Righteousness
No. 34—Baptism

The Sickle and Sharp Sickle sold only upon recommendation.

Five Years In Christian Science—cloth bound $1.60

Published and For Sale by

WILLIAM W. WALTER

564 New York Street **Aurora, Illinois**